Cultural
Anthropology
and
the
Old
Testament

Cultural Anthropology and the Old Testament

by
Thomas Overholt

Fortress Press
Minneapolis

Cultural Anthropology and the Old Testament

Library of Congress Cataloging-in-Publication Data

Overholt, Thomas W., 1935–
    Cultural anthropology and the Old Testament / by Thomas W. Overholt.
        p.   cm. — (Guides to biblical scholarship)
        Includes bibliographical references.
        ISBN 0-8006-2889-6 (alk. paper)
        1. Bible. O.T. —Criticism, interpretation, etc. 2. Ethnology in the Bible. I. Title II. Series
    BS661.O94 1996
    221.6′7—dc20   95-43457
                                                CIP

Manufactured in the U. S. A.   AF 1-2889

00   99   98   97   6   7   8   9   10

Contents

Editor's Foreword

The use of social-scientific theories and methods for the study of biblical texts and biblical issues has flourished in recent years, and it continues to do so. But the conversation between such approaches and biblical studies is by no means new. In many instances, as disciplines such as sociology and anthropology were defining themselves in the nineteenth century they were dealing with biblical materials or issues. Moreover, the boulevard between biblical studies and the social sciences was a two-way street. Max Weber, for example, both learned from the biblical scholarship of his day and developed his theories of society through the study of biblical texts. Closer to the topic of this book is the pioneering anthropological work of W. Robertson Smith and James G. Frazer.

Biblical studies have been influenced if not shaped by a wide range of explanations that have their roots in anthropology, for example, concerning the evolutionary stage of Israelite culture, the understanding of particular offices or roles, and the interpretation of symbolic language. But in recent years most of those venerable theories have been seriously reevaluated, if not discarded altogether.

Anthropology has been and continues to be understood in various ways. Physical anthropology, the investigation of the evolution and development of the human species, hardly comes into play in this context. But the other side of the discipline, generally understood as cultural anthropology, covers a wide range of approaches. It is closely related to ethnology, the study and analysis of particular cultures, as well as to archaeology, history, and sociology. Structural approaches have found a home in the discipline under the leadership of such scholars as Claude Lévi-Strauss and Edmund Leach.

As employed by Overholt, anthropology entails the comparative analysis of cultures, with particular emphasis on such issues as social roles and religious systems. Thus it is a cross-cultural enterprise that entails the development of categories for understanding that illuminates patterns of human activity. The goal is to better comprehend a particular culture by seeing it in the broader context of similar human activities. Since human actions are always understood in communal contexts, one might well call this approach socio-cultural anthropology.

Overholt has been a pioneer in the integration of anthropological theories, methods, and data with biblical studies. He has made particular contributions in the use of comparative data from Native North American cultures, and has focused especially on the understanding of religious specialists such as prophetic figures. In using these materials he is more concerned with cultural features as dynamic than as static phenomenon, showing how social roles and cultural symbols change over time.

In this volume Overholt first sets out an understanding of anthropological method in relationship to the Old Testament and then applies the approach to a range of biblical texts and issues. He does not argue that anthropology should replace other methods of study, but that it should be used in conjunction with both traditional scholarship and other emerging approaches. The value of anthropology, he argues, is that it helps to overcome the distance of time, geography, and culture between the contemporary reader and the biblical world. The biblical scholar as anthropologist asks questions that the authors and tradents of the biblical texts either took for granted or were not concerned to reflect upon, especially issues of the social organizations and dynamics in which they were immersed. Thus anthropology can enable the modern student to better interpret both the biblical texts and their cultural contexts.

—GENE M. TUCKER

Preface

A preface affords one an opportunity to say thank you and to reflect. I am grateful to three undergraduate students—Tom Janikowski, Debra Maier, and Crystal Voigt—who read and discussed with me drafts of the first two chapters. Their comments and criticisms were constructive in the best sense of that word, and helped me make significant improvements in the manuscript. I also received helpful comments from Barbara Butler and Alice Keefe, colleagues at the University of Wisconsin—Stevens Point, and from Carol Meyers, Paula McNutt, James Flanagan, and Frank Frick, who read the portions of chapter 3 that summarize their work. Gene Tucker encouraged me to undertake writing this volume and provided me with helpful comments and skilled and timely editing along the way to its completion. Thanks to all. As the saying goes, the errors remain mine, but any praise is partly theirs.

Two reflections: On the occasion of publishing a volume in the Guides to Biblical Scholarship series, it seems appropriate to recall that J. Coert Rylaarsdam, the first editor of the Old Testament volumes in the series, was my advisor at Chicago more than thirty years ago and is the person most responsible for my decision to make a career of Old Testament studies. It has proved to be a good choice, and I remember him with gratitude. I think also of one of those fortuitous benefits of belonging to a scholarly community. Prof. Francis Landy chanced to hear a paper I read at an annual meeting of the Society of Biblical Literature and suggested that I look up Geoffrey Samuel's *Mind, Body and Culture: Anthropology and the Biological Interface,* a book that proven important to my thinking about the subject of this volume.

I dedicate this book to Robert P. Carroll, a scholar with whom I frequently argue, precisely for that reason. In recent years my disagreements with him have led me to rethink and, I hope, clarify my own views on biblical prophecy. He is a kind, but tough-minded critic, and I value his comments.

I

Cultural Anthropology and the Old Testament

The Bible has been one of the core documents of Western culture. It has been valued over the centuries by many different people and groups and interpreted in a variety of ways. Particularly since the mid-nineteenth century, it has been the subject of critical examination by scholars, and a glance at the titles of previous volumes in this series will suggest the variety of methods they have developed and refined for interpreting its contents. In this book I will explore how data and theories from anthropology can be useful additions to our repertoire of strategies for interpreting the Old Testament.

Broadly speaking, anthropology is the study of human beings in the context of the groups in which they live and interact.[1] Historically, anthropologists have focused their attention on cultures other than and often distant from their own. One of the stock-in-trade methodological tools of anthropology as a discipline has been fieldwork characterized by participant observation: researchers take up residence in a society for an extended period, record some segment of what goes on there, and attempt to describe in terms familiar to their own culture "the general features of social life" they have observed (Geertz 1983, 58). Researchers in ethnohistory, one of the subdisciplines within the field of anthropology, make extensive use of written records.

There is, of course, no possibility of our being participant observers in ancient Israelite society. Rather, we will be using ideas and data that derive from the work of anthropologists to help us interpret texts from the ancient past. Two kinds of benefit may result from using anthropological methods and materials. On the one hand, fieldwork reports will prove to be rich sources of comparative materials for helping us to understand specific phenomena, such as holy men who heal the sick and raise the dead. On the other hand, theoretical constructs developed by anthropologists provide insights into the nature of society and social processes and can be valuable in our attempts to interpret ancient texts.

Do we need the assistance of yet another method of interpretation? Consider the following story about the prophet Elisha:

> In those days Elisha regularly passed through the village of Shunem on his travels, and a wealthy woman who lived there suggested to her husband that they build a small chamber on the roof of their house and offer it as accommodation to the wandering "holy man of God." During one of his visits, Elisha summoned the woman and inquired what he might do for her in return for all the trouble she had gone to on his behalf. She lacked neither wealth nor status, but she was without children and her husband was old. Elisha promised that she would conceive and bear a son, and, so the story goes, she did.
>
> One day, when the child was older, he went into the countryside to join his father and the reapers, and here he became ill. He was taken home, where he died in his mother's arms. She placed her son's corpse on the prophet's bed, summoned a servant and donkey, and, brushing aside her husband's question ("Why go to him today? It is neither new moon nor sabbath"), went quickly to Mount Carmel to find the man of God. Seizing Elisha's feet, she did not tell him of her son's death, but accused him of having deceived her. In response Elisha gave his servant, Gehazi, his staff and instructed him to go quickly to the woman's house and place it on the child's face. Then, at her urging he himself followed her home.
>
> When Elisha arrived and found the child dead, he went into the chamber, closed the door, and prayed to Yahweh. He then stretched himself out on top of the corpse, which slowly revived. Summoning the woman, he presented her with a living son. She "fell at his feet, bowing to the ground." (2 Kgs. 4:8–37)

Many stories in the Hebrew Bible, at least on first reading, give us the illusion that things are "normal" and understandable, but the tale of Elisha and the Shunemite woman is not one of them. To state only the most obvious point, the narrative assumes a world in which holy men cure infertility with a word and resuscitate the dead by ritualized physical contact; this does not correspond to the world as we moderns experience it. If our goal is to understand such a story, we will need to supplement the usual range of critical tools used in biblical studies.

The problem facing us as we read and study this story is how to interpret material that has its roots in a different culture and seems strange to persons from our own. Anthropologists routinely face the same difficulty, though the data they puzzle over most often come from contemporary cultures and more recent texts rather than an ancient culture and its texts. Anthropologists attempt to gain knowledge of the way people in other times and cultures think, feel, and imagine. As Clifford Geertz puts it, they seek knowledge of "what the devil [these people] think they are up to." For Geertz, the effort to grasp concepts that arise from the experience of people in another culture but are unfamiliar in our own involves the attempt to interpret their symbol systems. Insofar as such attempts are successful, the results will have something in common with "grasping a proverb, catching an allusion, seeing a joke" (1983, 56–68, 69–70). Anthropologists are often quite good at this, and I will argue that their insights into a range of human experiences can often be put to good use by students of the biblical literature.

Chapters 2 and 3 will lay out specific examples of how one might put into practice this approach to the biblical materials. The structure of chapter 2 reflects the two kinds of benefits mentioned earlier. The first section, "Elijah and Elisha as Men of Power," draws heavily on anthropological field studies to suggest a context in which to interpret some of the more puzzling features of the stories about these two prophets. The second section, "Elijah and Elisha in Israelite Society," uses anthropological theory to understand the dynamics of the society in which they operated. For the moment, however, this practical application must remain a promise while we attend to some preliminary matters, beginning with a characterization of what I have been calling "anthropological theory."

THE USEFULNESS OF ANTHROPOLOGICAL THEORY

To interpret an Old Testament text requires that one attempt to view it in its ancient context—in the case of 2 Kings 4, the history, culture, and society of monarchic Israel. Neither this society nor any other was (or is) a stable and homogeneous entity. Societies are composed of numerous individuals and groups, each with a potentially different way of understanding, valuing, and acting on the legacy of culture that they all in some sense share, and each of these ways is subject to change over time. Anthropological theory can offer valuable assistance by helping us understand the nature of culture and of the relationship between a given culture and the everyday lives of the individuals who live in it.[2]

There is a long-standing debate among anthropologists about how culture is to be defined. I offer here a definition from Clifford Geertz that will be useful for our purposes: culture is "an historically transmitted pattern of meanings embodied in symbols, a system of inherited conceptions expressed in symbolic forms by means of which men communicate, perpetuate, and develop their knowledge about and attitudes toward life" (1973, 89). Put another way, culture consists of "webs of significance" that humans themselves spin and in which they are suspended. The analysis of these webs is, therefore, "an interpretive [enterprise] in search of meaning" (5).

Starting from this understanding of culture (others would be possible), we are prompted to address certain questions to a text. To revert momentarily to the story of Elisha and the Shunemite woman, we might ask: What is the pattern of meanings contained in this account of resuscitation? What are the prominent symbolic forms encountered in it? What knowledge about and attitudes toward life are displayed? That satisfactory answers to these questions are not immediately apparent illustrates Geertz's notion that the major obstacle to people from one culture comprehending what people from another culture "are up to is . . . a lack of familiarity with the imaginative universe" they have created and in terms of which they understand and organize their lives (1973, 13).

The point of an appeal to theory is to help us think more clearly about such matters. Attention to theory should also result in an awareness of ongoing discussions and debates among anthropologists. This should have the salutary effect of warning us against uncritical dependence on studies based on outmoded or controversial presuppositions, such as an evolutionist theory according to which all societies pass through identical stages of development (see Rogerson 1978, 12–16). The methodological guidelines suggested by Robert R. Wilson in an earlier volume in this series are an attempt to avoid this and similar pitfalls (Wilson 1984, 28–29).[3]

There is, however, no single theory on which most anthropologists agree. To the contrary, Stanley Barrett (1984, chaps. 1 and 2) points out that over the years literally dozens of "theoretical orientations" toward the subject matter and methodology of the field have developed. Among these are structural functionalism (focusing on social structure, which largely determines individual behavior), historical particularism (focusing on specific culture areas—such as the Northwest Coast of North America—and seeing diffusion of traits as the key to reconstructing a culture's history), culture and personality (stressing individual personality structure as the key to understanding a particular culture), and cultural materialism (offering a modern version of evolutionist theory). Barrett argues that despite this variety, anthropological theory has been "non-cumulative": "little significant advance" has occurred since the work of the early theorists Karl Marx, Max Weber, and Emile Durkheim.

In the face of this plurality, which position should a student of biblical literature adopt? The fact that there is no obvious consensus among anthropologists invites us to be eclectic, carefully choosing theoretical insights that seem useful for explaining the particular texts on which we are currently focusing. To borrow words from the conclusion of a recent and particularly useful reworking of anthropological theory: "I do not believe that it is possible to establish that any theory is the 'best' available except in a limited and provisional sense. 'Best' . . . can only mean 'best out of what we have available at present for the particular purposes and demands that we have in mind'" (Samuel 1990, 164). In this sense the "best" theory will account for the data in a text in a way that seems to enhance our understanding of it.

Still, to be eclectic does not imply that one must know about and give equal weight to the whole range of anthropological theories. One will inevitably gravitate to the authors one finds most persuasive. In addition, one's confidence will be strengthened by discovering theoretical positions that, though conceptually different, are nevertheless congruent in important respects. For example, the writers I have found most useful generally agree (1) that in order to understand how societies work it is necessary to take into account both agency (that is, individual human action) and social structure; (2) that social life is by nature contradictory; and (3) that it is necessary to operate with a nonpositivist epistemology which holds that anthropological description does not so much mirror social reality as provide one of several possible maps that can guide us in our attempts to understand society. Let me elaborate on each of these points.

Agency and Structure

For the most part, our everyday experiences suggest that individual human beings, though powerfully influenced by the cultural patterns of the societies in which they live, are nevertheless able to make choices and act independently. Sometimes such independence takes the form of rebellion against certain norms of society, but even the actions of the more acquiescing often deviate from these norms. An understanding of this basic social process will help us interpret the dynamics of stories like those in the Elijah and Elisha cycle.

Stanley Barrett points out that there is an ambiguous relationship between beliefs based on societal norms and individual actions, "between what people say and what they do, between formal and informal codes of behavior" (1984, 23–24). From his perspective, the underlying cause of this ambiguity in society is that "contradiction is a central characteristic of our behavior." It is not just that humans, though shaped by the norms of their societies, spend considerable energy "breaking, bending, and twisting" those norms. At every level of behavior, from individual choices to involvement in complex social organizations, people are confronted by contradictory values and norms and, as often as not, possess no unambiguous criteria for deciding among them. Yet, despite this, "people not only choose and act but do so in a consistent, patterned manner" (146, 174).

Geoffrey Samuel provides us another way of conceptualizing this interplay of agency and structure. According to Samuel, "informal knowledge"—that is, "the knowledge that is implicit in our daily activities, in the collection of techniques, information, and ways of behaving that we use to carry on the business of living"—forms one of the basic components of human social life. Some of this knowledge (for example, the route from my house to the grocery store) relates to the mind. Some of it (for example, how to ride a bicycle) relates to the body. Taken as a whole, the informal knowledge possessed by individual persons constitutes "a patterning of mind and body as a totality." Individuals will obviously differ in the informal knowledge they possess. As a result, there will be, within the cultural constraints that are a part of life in any society, a variety of ways of "operating successfully in the world" (1990, 5–6).

Samuel rejects the idea of a dichotomy between the individual and society. Instead, both individuals and societies operate within a "general unstructured field" in which a number of options exist for "the patterning of relationships" among human beings, plants, animals, and the physical environment. He calls this general field the "social manifold" and the options that exist within it "modal states." Both structure and individual agency are operative within the social manifold, the former because at a given point only "a limited repertoire of individual modal states" is available and the latter because individuals can "switch between available states" in their repertoires, or create new ones, in response to situations they encounter (Samuel 1990, 10–14).[4]

This conception adds a further dimension to Geertz's description of culture as a series of webs of significance that humans themselves spin and in which they are suspended. Observing that "these webs are neither purely individual (once spun, they take on a life of their own) nor . . . purely social (they have spinners)," Samuel suggests we should look for "some kind of conceptual space, itself neither individual nor social, within which the webs have their existence." What the web metaphor leaves out of account is the flow of time within which "these processes of spinning and being caught" occur. To take this dimension into account, Samuel proposes another metaphor: the "structures of meaning and feeling in which and through which we live" can be seen "as patterns formed by currents in the course of a vast stream or river" (1990, 11).

Samuel's elaboration of this metaphor is worth quoting:

> As individual human beings and as members of social groups, we are not simply driven along blindly by the currents. We can orient ourselves in relation to them and steer ourselves to some degree in the direction that we prefer. We presumably have some ability to affect the flow through our actions. These currents, however, are the environment within which we move. They are the field of forces within which our activity takes place and we cannot step outside of them. For the most part, too, they are much bigger and stronger than we are, at least as individuals. . . . We need to remember, however, that the currents cannot ultimately be separated from the individuals who both constitute them and *are constituted by them.*
>
> We might describe the 'substance' within which this flow takes place as something like 'relatedness' or 'connectedness' (1990, 12).

Individual modal states have a number of features. They provide patterns in terms of which persons can understand the flow of their experiences. They correspond to "specific moods, motivations, feelings and emotions," as well as to "a particular subjective sense of self and a particular way" of perceiving one's "relationship to other individuals and other aspects of the environment" (see Samuel 1990, 71–74).

That several different conceptual frameworks can exist "within a single social context" is explained by the fact that individuals may have different "internal representations" of that context. Individuals internalize the "modal states of the manifold" selectively. Not all members of a society "have the same set of states," and the states "are always in the process of change" (Samuel 1990, 61, 70–71).

Our discussion of "agency and structure" has required us to consider the interrelationship of three things: culture, a set of patterns or webs that in Geertz's terms are "the fabric of meaning in terms of which human beings interpret their experience and guide their action"; social structure, the specific forms that such actions take; and individuals, with their own peculiar funds of knowledge and motivations (cf. Geertz 1973, 145). Geertz (1973, 142–69) argues that tensions or discontinuities among these three provide the primary forces that drive social change; he illustrates this point with a case study of a Javanese funeral ritual that was disrupted as a result of changes in social structure that rendered traditional cultural patterns ambiguous and in turn affected the actions of the participants.[5]

Views about the complex interrelationship between individual action and social structure such as those just discussed are not isolated and idiosyncratic. In a major review of recent anthropological theory, Sherry Ortner identifies an emerging focus on "practice" which accepts the three-sided proposition "that society is a system, that the system is powerfully constraining, and yet that the system can be made and unmade through human action and interaction" (1984, 158).

Nor is this view confined to anthropologists. In a way analogous to Samuel's view, the sociologist Anthony Giddens refuses to make either social institutions or human agents the focus of social theory. Social life as we in fact experience it is "recursive" in nature:

> When I pursue the activities of my daily life, I draw chronically upon established convention—in a manner which is both largely tacit and at the same time extraordinarily complex—in order to do so. But this very process of drawing upon convention reconstitutes it, in some part as binding influence upon the behaviour of others as well as that of myself. My activities are thus embedded within, and are constitutive elements of, structured properties of institutions stretching well beyond myself in time and space. (1987, 11)

In subsequent chapters we will turn to the examination of specific Old Testament texts, but at this point we can at least note that judging the relationship of social structure to individual agency has also been a problem for readers of the Old Testament. The seemingly dominant Yahwistic "faith of Israel" does not always square with activities reported of specific Israelites. The Elisha resuscitation narrative is a dramatic case in point, as is the ambivalence about divination, which is both condemned and rather routinely practiced (see chapter 3). The theoretical understanding of the relationship between structure and agency that I have been exploring can contribute to a more nuanced view of these tensions within Israelite society.

The Contradictoriness of Social Life

The contradictory nature of social life is already evident in the views just surveyed on the dialectic between human action and social restraint. Of these, it is Barrett who focused attention most specifically on "the contradictory nature both of our conceptual schemes and of our behaviour" (1984, 146). Contradiction, which he distinguishes from conflict by restricting it "to a single unit, whether an individual actor, an institution, or an entire social formation" (147), is present at the "micro" level (for example, an individual facing the demands of two roles, like spouse and parent), the "middle" level (for example, a university balancing its missions to teach and to do research), and the "macro" level (for example, the classic contradiction of bourgeoisie and proletariat in capitalist society) of society (147–72). If it appears less evident at the latter two, that is because at these levels "moral communities have sprung up around particular sides of contradictions" and conflict has arisen between these communities. In short, "choice no longer is an existential problem for the individual," who at these levels is "cloaked in normative attire, and structured into and out of certain kinds of behaviour by virtue of the properties of the institutional sphere" (147).

In a similar vein, Geertz speaks of "an inherent incongruity and tension between" culture ("an ordered system of meaning and of symbols, in terms of which social interaction takes place") and social structure ("the pattern of social interaction itself"), as well as between both of these and what he calls "personality structure" ("the pattern of motivational integration within the individual"). The discontinuities among these elements provide "some of the primary driving forces in change" (1973, 144–45).

Barrett identifies a number of "neutralizing mechanisms" that "conceal and neutralize contradiction, and in this way add to the complexity of the social realm" (1984, 177). These include humankind's "felt need for control, order, and predictability"; the weight of habit and convention; the illusory "simplified image of the world" that we adopt in order to "retain [our] sanity"; rituals that are intended "to smooth over contradiction and to elevate acts into the realm of moral sanctity, to render them as ends not subject to evaluation"; and ideology, which can be used by the power elite "to render the masses inert." Most important is the "role of the power elite" and the "weight of the existing institutions of society," which "press behaviour into a particular mode and reproduce the conditions that perpetuate them" (177–88).

"Map" versus "Mirror"

In one of his essays Jonathan Smith uses "map" as a metaphor for religion (1978, 289–309). Maps employ arbitrarily selected conventions in the service of presenting an ordered view of a particular territory. By analogy, this is also the function of religion, which Smith describes as "one mode of constructing worlds of meaning, worlds within which men find themselves and in which they choose to dwell" (290). Samuel presses the map metaphor into service in order to distinguish between the "new epistemologies" (there are many ways to map a territory, depending upon which aspects one selects) and the empiricist/positivist tradition in which scientific knowledge and theories were considered to be value-free (1990, 20–21). In a similar fashion Geertz speaks of a blurring of genres in contemporary social thought, a blurring that is symptomatic of "not just another redrawing of the cultural map . . . but an alteration of the principles of mapping" (1983, 20). He points out that some assumptions that have been central to the social sciences—for example, that brute facts exist and that it is possible and desirable to create "a formal vocabulary of analysis purged of all subjective reference"—are being challenged, and that explanation is now regarded more as a matter of interpreting the sense of actions than of specifying the causes of behavior (34).

When we turn to anthropology for assistance in interpreting biblical texts, our goal will not be to establish a normative pattern that mirrors Israelite society. Rather, we will employ ethnographic examples and anthropological theory to help us construct a "map" of the social and religious situation reflected in particular texts. I will demonstrate that this mapping convention is useful in helping us interpret these texts, but I will not claim that it is the only, or the definitive, way their "territory" can be mapped.

One final point: John Rogerson (1989, 26) and others speak of the limits of anthropology based on "incomplete historical records." In terms of this book, the problem is how one can apply anthropological methods and materials in a study of ancient texts. Gillian Feeley-Harnik, an anthropologist, does not think this is a major issue, since data derived from live informants are beset by problems like those derived from ancient texts. The main thing is the questions one brings to the study: "As Marc Bloch once said, 'A document is a witness; and like most witnesses, it does not say much except under cross-examination. The real difficulty lies in putting the right questions.' Precisely the same is true of ethnographic research, where the laconic reply is usually, 'It's custom.'" Interpreters of biblical texts can certainly sympathize with her observation that "there is never enough evidence, precisely because the questions change, provoking the search for more" (1982, 97–99).

PATTERN VERSUS PARTICULARITY

When we seek to bring material from one culture to bear on phenomena in another, we are employing a comparative approach. A standard objection to such an undertaking is that it risks submerging the particularity of the specific cultures in a sea of sterile generalization. Robert Carroll expresses this sentiment when he describes Old Testament prophecy as "an activity carried on among and between people within a specific society and conforming to the social norms operative among such people." He objects to comparative approaches, asserting that any "proper social analysis of prophecy" would concern itself with "the structures and values of ancient Israelite society" (1989, 203–04).

In his view, the main problem with recent "sociological analyses" of the prophets is that "theoretical models" such as they propose cannot compensate for "the lack of clear biblical data or override the ideological controls on those data," but succeed only in "producing a pattern of behaviour [which] ruin[s] the particularity of the data under scrutiny and thereby fail[s] to do justice to the texts" (1989, 220). The treatment of the Elijah and Elisha narratives in chapter 2 will show that Carroll overstates his case on both counts: We do possess data that are sufficiently distinct ideologically to be suitable for analysis, and this analysis enhances rather than ruins the particularity of the texts. Nevertheless, Carroll raises an important issue that we must address.

From one perspective, the overriding interest of twentieth-century anthropology, with its emphasis on fieldwork among specific peoples, has been to describe cultures in their particularity. The concern was not "with broad generalizations, but with the detailed study of individual societies. . . . Social anthropology saw itself as essentially descriptive, its task being to describe the structures of societies where such evidence was available. It did not see its task as the reconstruction of the origin and history of human institutions and religious beliefs" (Rogerson 1978, 17).

Geertz, though he is not entirely consistent on this matter, makes a similar point when he insists that sacred symbols are culturally specific (1973, 126–31). In another essay he speaks of the "particularity of the impact of religious systems upon social systems (and upon personality systems) which renders general assessments of the value of religion in either moral or functional terms impossible" (122). In his view the goal of "interpretive anthropology" is the "difficult achievement of seeing ourselves amongst others, as a local example of the forms human life has locally taken, a case among cases, a world among worlds" (1983, 16).

Nevertheless, anthropologists have been willing to suggest theories of culture and cultural change that apply across boundaries separating individual groups. Even in Geertz, one catches a glimpse of this other side. In the essay "Found in Translation," Geertz puzzles over "a riddle quite as irresolvable as it is fundamental: namely that the significant works of the human imagination . . . speak with equal power to the consoling piety that we are all like to one another and to the worrying suspicion that we are not." What we have to get straight is "how the massive fact of cultural and historical particularity comports with the equally massive fact of cross-cultural and cross-historical accessibility" (1983, 41–42). Apparently, both the particularity of specific cultures and more general patterns intelligible across cultural lines must be taken into account.

Models

One way of taking both these elements into consideration is to employ models. Models are theoretical constructs for mapping the world of our experience, and each represents one of a variety of possible ways of viewing that world (Samuel 1990, 68). Samuel, who finds models useful, stresses that individual societies differ from each other in many ways; "what they have in common is at a fairly abstract level" (109). Models are good for setting out the essential features of a particular kind of society or phenomenon and for describing how it works. It follows that they are also good for specifying the differences between types of phenomena. Samuel's discussion of the different "mechanisms . . . which operate on and transform the modal states" in traditional societies characterized by "the shamanic pattern," in contrast to modern industrialized societies characterized by the "rationalized pattern" of organization, illustrates both these functions (144–45). Because models provide us with a general picture, they should also sharpen our perception of the special features of any particular culture or group.

It is significant that in the same essay in which Geertz insists that sacred symbols are culturally specific, he suggests that the dynamics of the particular kind of symbol-making he describes are virtually the same in all cultures: no examples have been found, he tells us, of a people who have not produced a synthesis of "world view and ethos" (1973, 127).[6] Similarly, he argues in another place that while the content of "common sense" differs from culture to culture, it is possible to characterize common sense "transculturally" in terms of "its stylistic features."[7] To give one more example, in the context of a discussion of charisma Geertz says, "The relevance of historical fact for sociological analysis . . . rests on the perception that though both the structure and the expressions of social life change, the inner necessities that animate it do not" (1983, 142–43). The essay argues that there is both a need to legitimate power and a structural similarity in the way this is accomplished, both of which cross cultural lines. The cross-cultural focus of the discussion is well illustrated by his examples of symbolic forms by which a "governing elite" expresses "the fact that it is in truth governing"—"crowns and coronations, limousines and conferences" (1983, 124). These all seem to amount to models that operate on the principle that by concentrating on broad patterns of behavior we can look beyond culturally specific details and learn something significant about important social processes.[8]

Later in the essay mentioned above, Carroll says, "One definition of the prophetic role which seems to attract a number of analysts and make for agreement between them . . . is the notion of the prophet as the speaker of the divine word with reference to the future" (1989, 214). The "role in Israelite society" this posits "has the advantage of settling for the lowest common denominator with which virtually no scholar can disagree," but it may also "make biblical prophecy equivalent to diviners, magicians, witches, soothsayers and other mantic roles found in most societies. It also puts the emphasis on the spoken utterance in the role of prophet and thereby ignores the actor-visionary aspects included in the biblical traditions" (214–15). Carroll's tone is negative; such a model is, he claims, too general to be useful in distinguishing the character of prophecy from other phenomena. But without endorsing this particular model, I suggest that its putative failure to separate prophets from diviners may tell us something important about prophecy, namely that the social dynamics of prophecy and divination are not in fact so different as biblical scholars have traditionally held them to be (see Overholt 1989, 117–47, and chapter 3 below).

In an essay in which she examines the issue of slavery with special reference to Paul's letter to Philemon, Gillian Feeley-Harnik suggests that cross-cultural comparison involves "the comparison of whole systems rather than bits and pieces, with due regard for the social and cultural circumstances in which they were collected and analyzed." Its purpose "is not to swamp the distinctive features of cultural and social life in the common mind of humanity . . . but rather to bring them more sharply into focus. By exposing researchers to the wide range of issues that may be raised by similar questions in different contexts, while simultaneously extricating them from the social and cultural circumstances that normally provide answers, a cross-cultural perspective helps to focus attention on the particular variables that may be relevant to understanding in any special case" (1982, 100).

Cross-Cultural Comparison

Cross-cultural comparison is legitimate and can lead to useful results. Behind the matters we have been discussing lurks a challenge to that view, however, and it is necessary to explore some of the objections that have been raised.

Joanne Waghorne argues that in Geertz's essay, "Thick Description," comparison, though never specifically named as such, is viewed as "the chief methodological obstacle to the development of a sophisticated ethnography." This is because "as a method of analysis . . . [comparison] has tended to value the form over substance, the general at the expense of the particular, and the system above the subject" (1984, 36). Against this view, Geertz holds that the concepts animating a given culture are never free from their particular expressions in behavior, and therefore cannot be isolated and studied as universal phenomena (1984, 41–42). In Waghorne's view, this "obsession with particularity and diversity" shifts attention "from the search for the universals in the various symbol systems" and constitutes "a serious revolt against the base logic of the comparative method" (39).

This challenge, which we have already encountered, might be stated as follows, The culture of any particular group of people consists of "an historically transmitted pattern of meanings embodied in symbols" (Geertz 1973, 89). It incorporates "a multiplicity of complex conceptual structures" that are known through the behavior ("symbolic action," action that "signifies") of members of the group. Culture is an "acted document [and] thus is public . . . though ideational, it does not exist in someone's head." Therefore, any interpretation of a culture will have to be based on a "thick description" of the behavior of members of that culture.[9]

If one accepts Geertz's definition of culture, as I am inclined to do, then this is a forceful argument for making a particular society and its texts both the starting point and central focus of one's study. This starting point and focus, however, does not rule out cross-cultural comparison as a useful tool of interpretation along the lines suggested above in the discussion of models. Geertz himself takes for granted the utility of comparison in "providing out-of-the-way cases" that set "nearby ones in an altered context" (1983, 77).

Jonathan Smith has posed questions not so much about the legitimacy of comparison—a process he considers "a fundamental characteristic of human intelligence" without which "we could not speak, perceive, learn, or reason" (1978, 240)—as about the various ways in which it has been done. In an early essay, the somewhat sarcastic Latin title of which translates "When you add a little to a little, the result will be a great heap" (1978; see 1982, 22), he identifies and describes "four modes or styles" that have been used in comparisons of "religious and cultural data": the ethnographic, encyclopedic, morphological, and evolutionary. In his view none of the four is entirely satisfactory.

In his 1982 essay Smith raises a version of the problem discussed above: while "comparison is, at base, never identity," in the enterprise of comparison "the issue of difference has been all but forgotten" (1982, 21). It is easy to make patterns; in order to be interesting, comparison must postulate difference and methodically manipulate this difference to answer the questions, how?, why?, and so what?" The solution to the problem, he says, lies not in more data, but in "theories and reasons" (35).

Although Smith does not propose his own theory, he provides an indication of the direction such a theory might take by reviewing what he calls "an historical proposal from within the morphological mode" (1982, 26), which he finds in the work of the Pan-Babylonian school of ancient Near Eastern scholarship that flourished earlier in this century. Although sometimes wrong on matters of fact and open to criticism for an overreliance on diffusion in their theory, these scholars made a significant step in the right direction by combining history and morphology in "a rich model of cultural tradition that has three levels": "world view" (that imposes uniformity and can be diffused), "culture complex" (the particular *Gestalt* of a given people in terms of which the diffused world view is modified), and "the linguistic manifestation of the interaction of these two" (which particularizes the modified world view). They attempted, among other things, to "ground comparison and patterns in a historical process . . . [and] to balance generalities and particularities in a structure which integrated both" (29).

In the ongoing debate over whether similarities between cultures are the result of diffusion (in which case historical processes are central) or of parallel development (in which case "ahistorical constructs such as the 'psychic unity of mankind'" are central), the theory proposed by the Pan-Babylonian school, and apparently endorsed at least in broad outlines by Smith, comes down on the side of the former.

One might ask whether the debate between these options really has to be resolved in favor of one or the other in order to make some constructive advance or to do useful work. The societies studied by anthropologists almost invariably have been influenced to some degree by Euro-Christian culture, so diffusion of ideas and forms is always a possibility. On the other hand, certain experiences (among them life crises, illness, and the occasional feeling that one is confronting forces both mysterious and beyond one's control) are common to humans of whatever society, and one can assume that every culture has found ways to come to terms with them. Recall, for example, Geertz's claim that the fusion of ethos and world view is apparently universal.

If one then raises the question of how a nonhistorical type—for example, the model of prophetic activity I proposed in an earlier publication (Overholt, 1989)—illuminates particular historical manifestations (for example, Elijah, Amos), the response would be that the prophetic process it describes seems a useful way of dealing with some of these experiences, at least in societies where there is a belief in supernatural powers that are both able and willing to have an effect on the worldly affairs of human beings (see Wilson 1980, 28–32). Whether in a given instance the origin of this pattern is independent invention, diffusion, or some part of the former modified by the latter is an interesting question, but one that in most cases cannot finally be resolved. The pattern can nevertheless be identified, and it is useful in characterizing an important social process and providing a kind of benchmark for recognizing the specific forms that process takes as a result of the particular culture complex. This is where historical particularity comes in.[10]

Yet another side of the matter must be considered. If comparison runs the risk of emphasizing the general at the expense of the specific, limiting oneself to a single culture risks the opposite. This is I. M. Lewis's complaint against the rigid distinctions anthropologists have drawn between spirit possession, spirit mediumship, and shamanism. Lewis argues instead that "all the features that have been distinguished as signifying separate phenomena associated with contrasting social formations (past and present) actually regularly occur together within a single cultural context" (1986, 84). He uses the Siberian term *shaman* to designate this religious role, and hopes that his discussion will "contribute to a more informed understanding of universal religious roles, which for too long have been treated as though they represented different species beyond the reach of effective comparative analysis" (93).[11]

The problem of the appropriate context for interpreting cultural phenomena, which we have been dealing with up to now in terms of individual society versus comparison among several societies, appears in a somewhat different form at the level of the scholarly enterprise itself. Here it can be expressed in the question, Who owns the text? We may illustrate this point by citing a particular case: my comparison of the biblical Jeremiah with the Seneca Indian prophet, Handsome Lake, whose teachings come down to us in a written version that dates from several decades after his death (Overholt 1986, 321–31; cf. Overholt 1989, 59–66).

The anthropologist A. F. C. Wallace has published widely on Handsome Lake. He has also developed a well-known theory of cultural revitalization, and has used Handsome Lake as an example of how the revitalization process works. Robert Carroll is aware of this, and takes the notion of revitalization as the key to interpreting Handsome Lake. Having made this move, he sees little similarity between Jeremiah and Handsome Lake. He observes, for example, that neither the prophet Jeremiah before nor the book of Jeremiah during the exile functioned "to revitalise Judean culture." This understanding in turn shapes his comments on my comparison of the two figures, since he assumes that I intend to make Jeremiah my "biblical model of a revitalisation movement" (Carroll 1989, 219–20). This misconstrues my argument; Carroll looked for the parallel between Jeremiah and Handsome Lake in one place, and I in another, namely the pattern of social interaction described in the model of the prophetic process referred to above. We have to use anthropological texts responsibly, but we are not limited to interpreting them as their major expositors among anthropologists do, or in any other single way. Wallace uses the Handsome Lake history and text as evidence for his theory, I for mine. The two are not necessarily incompatible, but neither are they the same.

Finally, one must acknowledge that within the communities of faith that accept the Hebrew Bible as scripture, engaging in cross-cultural comparisons may raise certain theological issues. The very process of using anthropological materials in the study of biblical texts implies that the phenomena the texts describe are not in any absolute way unique to the groups that produced the Bible.[12] In view of the fact that biblical laws, literary forms, social institutions, and the like have for many years been routinely compared with the same features in other ancient Near Eastern cultures, this is not an altogether new problem. Still, anthropological comparisons will inevitably raise new issues. In what follows, we will suggest the probability that Yahwism in the monarchic period contained elements we usually associate with the religion of nonliterate cultures. Moreover, we will call into question assumptions about the uniqueness of Israelite prophecy and the strict distinction between prophecy and divination. Such ideas clearly have implications for theology, but their consideration is beyond the scope of this book.

TEXT AND REALITY

Inasmuch as I am proposing an anthropological approach to Hebrew Bible texts, one more problem needs to be addressed before we can move on to actual examples of the method at work: To what extent can we assume that the biblical texts reflect social reality? As a result of the work of contemporary literary critics of several schools of thought, it is commonplace today to recognize that the act of reading is always a creative encounter between reader and text. John Barton provides an excellent historical illustration of the fact that people get what they are looking for when they read scripture. In *Oracles of God: Perceptions of Ancient Prophecy in Israel after the Exile* (1986) he argues that postexilic Jewish, as well as Christian, readers assumed a "bipartite" division of scriptures into Torah and Prophets ("any book with scriptural status outside the Pentateuch"; 44) and that in general what the prophetic books meant to readers depended on the "kinds of information people in fact turned to them to discover" (151). Typically, readers of this period sought four kinds of information from these books—ethical instruction, foreknowledge of the present day, a divine plan for history, and theological truths—and the results of their reading often bore little resemblance "to what prophecy had originally been" (269). Similarly, empirical studies of contemporary readers have shown how their cultural setting and the particular assumptions they bring to the text affect what they get out of it (cf. Leenhardt 1980). Thus, since readers shape the texts they read, the question we need to ask is whether there is some content *in* the text for them to shape.

We can see what is at issue here if we look at Robert Carroll's critique of sociological/anthropological approaches to Old Testament prophecy. Carroll observes that prophetic texts available to us in the Hebrew Bible are distanced from their original context in oral prophecy, first by being written down and also by being subject to an ongoing editorial process. They are basically *literary* texts, the "imaginative creations of their writers," and we have little information "about what the writer was doing when writing a particular document." Thus if we simply suppose that they reflect social reality, we are making an "illegitimate transfer of meaning." The general tenor of Carroll's attack on anthropological studies of Old Testament prophecy is that they do not treat the biblical data "with appropriate epistemological caution" (1989, 217)—in the end the biblical data will not sustain their theorizing.

While it is obvious that the transformation of speech into writing frees a text from its original context and launches it on a life of its own, the issue is the extent to which this event and the subsequent process of readers (or editors) deriving their own meaning from the text affects the hints about social situations contained in the words themselves. Carroll cites the stories of Bathsheba's public bathing (2 Sam. 11:2), the Shunemite woman's consulting Elisha after the death of her son (2 Kgs. 4:18–25), and Judith's seduction of Holofernes (Judith 8–14), and asks, "What social customs can reliably be argued for from all these biblical stories?" It is a rhetorical question, expecting the answer, "None whatsoever." "To suppose a realism to these stories beyond the conventions of . . . storytelling is an illegitimate transfer of meaning from story to social background" (1989, 206).

But this overstates the case. I know of no one who would claim that exhibitionism (with intent to seduce?) and actual seduction in the interest of gaining advantage over one's enemy reflect "normative . . . social behaviour" (1989, 206), though no doubt both occurred from time to time in ancient Israelite society (as well as every other society that has ever existed, including our own). In this sense Carroll's appeal to "conventions of storytelling" raises an important issue—since it is well known that fiction can be quite realistic. Bathsheba's rooftop bath makes a good story, but the apparent realism does not guarantee that the narrative reports an actual event. The object of using anthropology to assist in the interpretation of Old Testament texts is not, however, to argue that such narratives are historically accurate, let alone normative. What one looks for in the texts and seeks to understand is more basic patterns of behavior; for example, the consulting of a prophet in a case of illness (see chapter 2). The objective is not to establish "reality" in some positivistic sense—this or that actually happened—but to suggest a broader social reality that was a part of the context in which the texts were produced and that continues to be reflected in the texts, despite their subsequent literary history.[13]

We must, of course, try to guard against arbitrarily imposing an anthropological interpretation on a text. Biblical (and other) texts, so far removed from us in time, space, and conceptual orientation, can be, as Carroll says, "like a dark glass in which we see our own reflections more often than the social reality which produced [them]. . . . The manipulation of the data by social theories does not produce the kind of comprehensive knowledge which is required for a coherent, cogent account of biblical society" (1989, 220). Furthermore, whether one takes a literary or an anthropological approach, one has "to be very sensitive to the amount of ideological editing involved in the creation of the text, editing which regularly distorts the historical-social roots of the text" (221).[14]

These are good points, but again Carroll has stated the strongest position regarding sociological analysis in order to refute it. What if one is not after "a coherent, cogent account of biblical society" as a whole, but rather insight into discrete parts of that society? If the Bible is "a dark glass" or, as he suggests in the same context, "a broken glass producing a confusion of reflections" (1989, 221), then we will be grateful for small and provisional advances toward understanding it. The choice between literary, anthropological, and other methods is both/and, not either/or.

The broad issue underlying this discussion is the matter of reference, the problem of whether words have meanings that are anchored in the real world of our experience. A strong case can be made that they do. At a level even more basic than literary texts, the fact that humans are for the most part quite skilled at getting along in the societies in which they live requires that language relate in powerful ways to the external world. The sociologist Anthony Giddens attempts to explain this relationship by calling attention to what he calls practical consciousness, the human agents' "practical mastery of social relations" in everyday affairs. This practical consciousness (which he says "intervenes between the conscious and the unconscious") organizes much of what we do in our daily activities, assigning "meanings to words and actions that do not originate solely" in either the referent or in language codes, but also in "the 'procedures' which agents use in the course of practical action to reach 'interpretations' of what they and others do." Meanings are thus both contextual and procedural (the operation of the practical consciousness is characterized by a certain methodology), accounting for the fact that words which "taken in isolation or considered lexically seem to have only vague meanings" can be quite precise in use (1987, 62–63). Geertz's emphasis on culture as an "acted document" and the analysis of it as an interpretive search for meaning carry the same implication (1973, 5, 10).

This does not assume that every member of a group will find the exact same meaning in a particular string of words, but it does assume that both words and their interpretation are grounded in a concrete social interaction. If the context of the words we confront is a culture different from our own, that raises the problem to another level but does not alter the basic assumption. Language is still grounded in concrete social situations, but now anthropologists or biblical interpreters must attempt to grasp concepts used effortlessly and naturally by another people well enough to be able to figure out and give expression to, as Geertz puts it, "what the devil they think they are up to" (1983, 58). This is a difficult task, and in the end we will never be able to perform it perfectly. Our best results will have something of the nature of "grasping a proverb, catching an allusion, seeing a joke" (70).

If we move our attention specifically to texts, the situation does not change much. The assumptions embodied in expressive realism—that texts are timeless witnesses to the convictions of their authors and to their experiences as part of a particular culture at a particular time—have come under heavy attack. In the words of Catherine Belsey, the positions from which texts "are intelligible . . . are never single because they are always positions in specific discourses." While language "provides the possibility of meaning," it is constantly in flux. Therefore, "what is inherent in the text is a range of possibilities of meaning. Texts, in other words, are plural, open to a number of interpretations. Meanings are not fixed or given, but are released in the process of reading" (1980, 19–20). In the search for these meanings readers need to be on the lookout for the unspoken ideologies both of the text and of their own cultural position (cf. Phillips 1990, 25–28).

We can now raise again the question of the text's content. In language reminiscent of Geertz's reflections on how one comes to understand elements of another culture, Michael LaFargue argues that the fact we can speak of "getting" a joke suggests there is some "determinate 'substantive content'" for us to "get." We should not look for this content in a referent that exists in some absolute sense outside the text and its language. Rather, it is to be found in a "system whose key elements are: (a) the words of the text, in a determinate relation [to] each other and to (b) the determinate life-world of the text authors; [as well as] (c) the mind-set of the author." The latter includes the associations that images and words have for an author as well as, "linguistic and literary conventions governing his speech, the shape of his existential concerns, and his mode of engagement with his own text." As a result of these factors, an author sees "the elements of the text and of his life-world in determinate relationships to each other, and thereby gives the whole a determinate character" (1988, 341, 350–55). In other words, texts are shaped by the interplay of authors, who have particular mind-sets, with the social realities of their time and place and the rules of their language. Texts do not mirror social reality directly, but to the extent that we can discover their "determinate and particular" meaning (354), they need not leave us entirely in the dark.

The key point is that the social reality assumed by the text is likely to be more complex than it appears on the surface, and the process by which we seek to grasp it will require the use of a variety of tools—historical, sociological, anthropological, and literary.

CONCLUSION

What, then, is to be gained by reading Old Testament texts from a point of view informed by anthropology? It is certain that such an approach will not liberate us from dependency on other established methodologies for the study of texts. Nor will it necessarily be useful with every text. Interpreters should be opportunistic, using whatever combination of methods and theories seems genuinely helpful in addressing the particular problems they bring to the text.

One possible answer to the question about the use of anthropology comes from John Rogerson, who praises N. P. Lemche's *Early Israel* as "a model of how anthropology should be studied in regard to the Old Testament": It "can indicate the complexities of social organisation and indicate broadly what is possible and what is not. It cannot be a substitute for historical research." Rather, it will be of most use in supporting "positions that are derived from historical and textual studies" (Rogerson 1989, 28, 31). I would prefer a slightly stronger statement along the following lines:

Many things stand in the way of our understanding Old Testament texts. The most obvious is that they are so distant in time, space, and culture from even those who stand related to them through the millennia-spanning continuity of the Jewish and Christian religious traditions. There are other problems as well. The authors' interests and ours differ, so that we find little explicit treatment of social organization and dynamics. Like authors in all ages, they expressed points of view, but because they operated with editorial conventions different from those employed by modern historians (for example, they did not clearly identify their sources, they mingled "earlier" passages with "later" ones, and so on), and because of our scanty historical knowledge of the period, it is often difficult to sort out the ideologies and other cultural features that lie behind the production of a text. Our knowledge of the society that produced the Hebrew Bible contains serious, and sometimes large, gaps. It is hard to miss the irony here: We turn to anthropology because of the paucity of our information, but that very paucity makes the use of anthropology problematic.

Nevertheless, insights derived from anthropology can often allow us to make inferences that at least provisionally fill in some of these gaps. I have elsewhere attempted to do this with respect to certain features of the social dynamics of Old Testament prophecy, discussing such matters as the nature of prophetic authority and the function of miracles (Overholt 1989). In the following chapters I hope to provide additional examples of how this kind of undertaking can help us interpret biblical texts.

NOTES

1. The discipline of anthropology encompasses many different approaches to this study, each of which would have its own definition of the field. See, for example, Barrett's discussion of "the current state of anthropological theory" (1984, especially chaps. 1 and 2).

2. For an illuminating argument that "culture . . . is not just an ornament of human existence but . . . an essential condition for it," cf. Geertz 1973, 43–51.

3. D. Fiensy (1987) cautions that in using anthropological data, biblical scholars must be sensitive to the debates going on within the discipline of anthropology.

4. His technical term for this theoretical understanding of the interrelationships of mind, body, and culture is "multimodal framework."

5. For more on this ritual, see pp. 54 below.

6. Geertz defines "ethos" as a culture's "tone, character, and quality of . . . life, its moral and aesthetic style and mood," and "world view" as the "picture" that members of a culture share "of the way things in sheer actuality are, their concept of nature, of self, of society."

7. Geertz discusses five such features, including "naturalness" (common sense "represents matters . . . as being what they are in the simple nature of the case"; 85) and "immethodicalness" ("common-sense wisdom is shamelessly and unapologetically ad hoc," generating proverbs as inconsistent as "look before you leap" and "seize the day"; 90).

8. On the other hand, Geertz specifically criticizes Victor Turner's "social drama" model, both the strength and the weakness of which is that it can be

applied to many situations. "It can expose some of the profoundest features of social process, but at the expense of making vividly disparate matters look drably homogeneous" (1983, 28).

9. Cf. Geertz (1973, 3–30); the quotations in the last part of the paragraph are from p. 10.

10. Feeley-Harnik, who assumes "that the beliefs and practices of all human beings are fundamentally comparable" (1982, 126), sees cross-cultural comparison as a way to comprehend the differences of particular cultures.

11. Samuel also opts for a broad definition of shamanism. The shaman is a ritual specialist concerned with manipulating, balancing, and sometimes introducing new modal states. The Ndembu diviner is such a specialist (1990, 107).

12. This may be seen as an advantage. Chris Haur, Jr., comments, "the foremost reason [for employing anthropology in Old Testament studies] is that anthropology by its very nature enforces the criterion of cross-cultural validity upon its theories and concepts (as sociology and social psychology do not to the same degree). Thus we are provided with control upon the inevitable human inclination toward ethnocentrism" (1987, 16).

13. Indeed, it is extremely difficult to interpret a biblical text without making some suggestions about the broader social reality that lies behind its production or editorial transformation. Thus Carroll himself claims to detect "the interests concealed behind various levels of tradition in Jeremiah" (1986, 72; cf. 65–82) and to identify subtexts reflecting aspects of the social dynamics and ideology of the postexilic period (1991).

14. David Jobling puts the matter this way: In working with texts, one must be sensitive to their agendas (subtexts), to the potentially intricate play of subtexts in a given text, and to the occurrence of the same subtext in superficially unrelated texts. One must also avoid working "too near the text . . . .simply accept[ing] the Bible as evidential bedrock" (1991, 178, 180).

II

Interpreting Elijah and Elisha

The stories about Elijah and Elisha can be better understood if viewed in the light of insights from anthropology. In this chapter we will explore the implications of the points made in chapter 1 by taking a detailed look at some aspects of these narratives, especially the story of resuscitation with which we began. In chapter 3 we will explore how anthropology can illumine other texts and topics.

ELIJAH AND ELISHA AS MEN OF POWER

The account in 1 Kings 17:17–24 of how Elijah resuscitated a widow's dead son parallels the story about Elisha and the Shunemite woman (2 Kgs. 4:8–37). Both are part of a group of narratives about prophets, mostly Elijah and Elisha, that have been incorporated into the Deuteronomic historian's account of the reign of the Israelite kings from Omri to Jehu (found in 1 Kgs. 16:21–2 Kgs. 10:36). These narratives begin abruptly in 1 Kings 17:1 and flow almost without interruption until 2 Kings 8:15. Three stories separated from the rest, the anointing of Jehu (2 Kgs. 9:1–13) and events attending Elisha's death (13:14–19, 20–21), bring the cycle to a close. One striking feature of these stories is that they contain nearly all the accounts of miracles in the Hebrew Bible.[1]

The composite nature of this collection of narratives is widely recognized, and considerable energy and ingenuity have been devoted to reconstructing their literary history. Individual narratives have been dissected into original kernel and later additions.[2] The traditions of the two prophets have been analyzed individually,[3] and their combination into a single cycle of stories explained.[4] Some of the stories told about Elijah have parallels in the Elisha narratives, and literary studies have predictably sought to discern directions of dependence. There is no consensus on these matters.

If one temporarily sets aside these traditional historical-critical questions and reads through this collection of Elijah and Elisha narratives from a point of view informed by anthropology, one observes that it is dominated by stories of feeding and curing—resuscitation is, after all, the ultimate cure. As the cycle begins, Elijah, fleeing from Ahab, is fed first by ravens (17:2–7) and then by a widow, whom he subsequently feeds through a miraculous multiplication of her meager supply of meal and oil (17:8–16). After the contest at Carmel, he flees to Horeb, and is again fed, this time by a "messenger of Yahweh" (19:5–7). For his part Elisha supplies water for the people of Jericho (2:19–22) and the armies of the three kings (3:9–20), and later feeds a widow (4:1–7), a group of prophets (4:38–41), and a group of one hundred persons (4:42–44).

As to the cures, near the beginning of the cycle we encounter the story of how Elijah resuscitated the widow's son (17:17–24). Elisha performs a similar feat (4:8–37), and cures the Syrian commander, Naaman, of his leprosy as well (5:1–27). Furthermore, near the end of the collection is a story that specifically recalls Elisha's resuscitation of the Shunemite woman's son (8:1–6), and, as if that were not sufficient, the final episode recounts another resuscitation, this time of a corpse that merely came into contact with the dead Elisha's bones (13:20–21). These prophets are powerful persons indeed.

Food and Folklore

Anthropologists have long been interested in the narrative traditions of the people they studied, and folklore and anthropology are closely allied disciplines. Susan Niditch's volume in this series provides a detailed discussion of the implications of folklore studies for Old Testament interpretation.

From the point of view of folklore studies, the stories about Elijah at Wadi Cherith (1 Kgs. 17:2–7) and at Horeb (1 Kgs. 19:3–18) can be identified as traditional episodes of the type identified by Dorothy Irvin in her analysis of ancient Near Eastern texts and narratives in Genesis. Such an episode is a narrative unit characterized by a standard plot that is "traditional in the sense that it occurs over and over in the same national literatures, and even shows similarities between different literatures" (1978, 10). Like the Hagar stories in Genesis 16:1–14 and 21:9–21, these two stories about Elijah have the structure of "traditional epiphany episodes." They begin with a summoning act (Elijah is in danger and is sent by Yahweh to hide out by the Wadi Cherith, 17:2–5; Elijah, fleeing and dispirited, calls on Yahweh to take away his life, 19:4–5a), progress to a saving appearance (by ravens, 17:6a; by a "messenger of Yahweh," 19:5b,7), and culminate with aid being given (ravens bring food, 17:6ab; the messenger brings bread and water, 19:6,

8a). Irvin demonstrates that the messenger in the Genesis narratives of this type is really God (93–104), and the same seems true of 1 Kings 19:4–8.

Three other narratives—Elijah's multiplying the widow's meal and oil and Elisha's multiplying the widow's oil and feeding one hundred persons on twenty loaves of bread and some grain—are examples of a widely distributed folklore motif, "the inexhaustible food-supply" (D1652 in the Aarne-Thompson motif-index; Thompson 1955–58). In Native American stories, this motif occurs as an episode in a longer narrative. Typically, a traveler comes at the end of the day to a lodge where an old woman feeds him from a tiny kettle in which she boils, for example, a single grain of rice. During the preparation the traveler doubts his hunger will be satisfied; he subsequently eats from the kettle until he is full, but is unable to consume all its contents. Some of these narratives contain both an inexhaustible food-supply episode and a resuscitation episode.[5]

The miraculous nature of the events in these stories is enough to put the interpreter on guard. What do we learn from tales of this sort? Susan Niditch warns that when dealing with stories that fit known folklore types, "we should be extremely cautious in drawing historical fact from the tale"(1987, 2–3).[6] As an alternative, one might view such narratives as "expressing in symbolic language what is believed to be true about God (Rogerson 1978, 84)"[7]

If we are not looking for historical content, the presence of these patterned tales, including stories of resuscitation, suggests other questions: What is the conceptual horizon of such stories? In what social or cultural circumstances would the ideas they contain have credibility? Perhaps they should alert us to the presence of a somewhat different social and intellectual world than we are used to envisioning when we read these biblical books.[8] The accounts of healing and resuscitation offer us some insights into this world.

Resuscitation is a common theme in folklore from around the world.[9] "Orpheus" tales, in which a living human pursues the soul of a loved one to the land of the dead and attempts to bring it back to the place of the living, are but one example. Åke Hultkrantz has even argued that these narratives, widely distributed in Native North America and elsewhere and "everywhere surprisingly alike," "reflect, at bottom, a shaman seance whose aim it has been to restore to life a sick, unconscious person regarded as 'dead'" (1957, 34, 240).

Curing and Resuscitation

The Hebrew Bible has relatively little to say about the cause and cure of illness. Yahweh is sometimes said to send disease on individuals

(Num. 12:13) or to cure illnesses (2 Kgs. 20:5,8; Gen. 20:17; Pss. 103:3, 30:2, 41:4, 107:20). Mostly, however, medical language connected with Yahweh's activity is metaphorical, referring to the illness and healing of the nation (for example, Exod. 15:26; Hos. 5:13, 7:1, 11:3; Lam. 2:13; Isa. 57:18–19; Jer. 3:22, 30:17). There are a few references to physicians (Jer. 8:22; 2 Chron. 16:12), but no accounts of their methods. Priests were involved in the diagnosis of leprosy, declaring on the basis of an examination that a person was either clean or unclean (Leviticus 13). They also performed rituals that effected a leper's reincorporation into the community of the ritually pure (Leviticus 14), but priests seem to have had no curing function.[10]

The most explicit descriptions of cures are found in prophetic narratives. 2 Kings 20:1–11 does not mention the cause of Hezekiah's illness, but reports that he prayed to Yahweh, who decided to heal him. Isaiah conveyed this information to the king and also performed a therapeutic action, laying a clump of figs on the king's boil so that he might recover. The story about Naaman the leper goes further, assuming that "the prophet" is known to be a healer (2 Kgs. 5:3), and depicting Elisha as welcoming the opportunity to perform the cure so that Naaman "may learn that there is a prophet in Israel" (v. 8).[11] Contrary to Naaman's expectation that the procedure would involve a face-to-face meeting with the healer, who would call upon his God and wave his hand over the affected spot (v. 11),[12] Elisha instructs him through a messenger to bathe seven times in the Jordan (v. 10). Later in the same narrative we learn that the prophet can cause, as well as cure, disease (vv. 26–27). These two stories connect prophets with curing and represent them as employing specific therapeutic actions. The accounts of resuscitation give us additional details, but in doing so raise some problems of their own.

Critical opinions on the resuscitation stories range from those who believe that the two were originally independent (Hentschel 1977), to those who see the Elisha story in 2 Kings 4 as the basis for the much shorter account about Elijah in 1 Kings 17 (Fohrer 1957; Schmitt 1977; Rofé 1988, 132–35), to those who see dependence flowing from Elijah to Elisha (Kilian 1966). Hentschel (1977, 195–201) thinks that the story of Elisha's providing for the widow (2 Kgs. 4:1–7) is dependent on a similar story about Elijah (1 Kgs. 17:8–16).

Nor have form critics been unanimous in their assessment of these stories. Armin Schmitt, who has done detailed literary and form-critical analyses of both the resuscitation narratives, calls the Elijah story a "constructed prophetic narrative," and the Elisha story from which he believes it came simply a "prophetic narrative." The first of the "twelve distinct genres" that Alexander Rofé uses to classify prophetic narratives is the "short *legenda*," which he defines as a localized popular tale containing a single miracle and reflecting the fear and admiration of simple believers toward a holy man (1988, 16). According to Rofé, the Elisha resuscitation is a "literary elaboration" of such a legenda, and the Elijah story is an "ethical *legenda*" in which the miracle is "not intended to benefit any particular person or persons, but to increase and spread the belief in God, even among other nations" (127). Long (1984, 1991) doubts the utility of fine distinctions between genres, and suggests that most of the narratives are best understood as examples of the "prophetic legend," by which he means stories that focus "both the teller's and the reader's interest on wonderful attributes and miraculous action of God and his prophet" (1984, 181).

My reason for this brief foray into the history of interpretation is to make a single point: Several generations of critical scholarship on these prophetic narratives have yielded no consensus as to their composition and transmission. Long makes this point again and again, saying that such stories may have had a variety of social settings, about which we can know little. Instead, he regularly elects to examine the literary setting of the stories within the larger work of the Deuteronomic historian (for example, 1984, 16, 175). This is a move akin to attacks on the documentary hypothesis concerning the composition and transmission history of the Pentateuch (cf. Whybray 1987). The failure of older methods to produce consensus gives a certain impetus and legitimacy to other approaches, like one based on anthropological comparisons.

The resuscitation stories provide a distinct characterization of Elijah's and Elisha's activity. First of all, they focus on the intimate involvement of the "man of God" in the daily lives of individuals. A citizen offers accommodations to a wandering holy man (1 Kgs. 17:19; 2 Kgs. 4:8–10), and he offers special favors in return (4:11–14; cf. 17:10–16). In the case of Elisha, he promises pregnancy and the birth of a son (4:15–17). The Shunemite woman consults Elisha at a time of family crisis, though strangely she at best hints at her motivation, and does not explicitly reveal the particular goal of her visit (4:25b–30). In both cases the hosts hurl a personal accusation at the holy man (17:18; 4:28).

Furthermore, these stories (like 2 Kgs. 5:3) depict Elijah and Elisha as healers. In each case the holy man himself employs a therapeutic procedure, in the process calling upon God, and effects a cure (17:21–22; 4:33–35). The cure is pictured as a resuscitation (17:23; 4:35). Elisha even undertakes a therapeutic procedure by proxy, using his servant and his staff (4:29,31). During the course of their curing activity, both men direct accusations of their own at Yahweh (17:20;

4:27). After the cure, people stand in awe of their power. The Elijah story includes an explicit confession of faith (17:24); in the other the response of the woman is to fall at Elisha's feet, "bowing to the ground" (4:37). Finally, Elisha seems to have been involved in regular communal rituals (4:23; "new moon," "sabbath").

At the same time, the language of the Elijah and Elisha narratives strongly reflects three assumptions compatible with the Deuteronomic ideology that is so dominant in the historical books of the Hebrew Bible: First, Yahweh has control over nature and history (he sends rain, 1 Kgs. 18:1, and famine, 2 Kgs. 8:1; he selects kings, 2 Kgs. 9:3). Second, when disaster strikes, it is interpreted as a punishment for human misbehavior (drought, 1 Kgs. 18:17–18; illness, 2 Kgs. 1:3–4). Third, the prophets are Yahweh's spokesmen, confronting kings and announcing Yahweh's intentions (1 Kgs. 18:1, 19:15–18; 2 Kgs. 1:16, 3:16–19, 7:1). The language of this set of assumptions is likely to seem somehow natural to us, reflecting as it does what we have come to see as important elements of preexilic Yahwism.

If we now consider the resuscitation stories' characterization of Elijah and Elisha in light of these Deuteronomic assumptions, we can observe that the two are not in complete harmony. In fact, the stories stand in tension with the Deuteronomic ideology at four important points. Moreover, these tensions stem from the fact that implicit in the stories is another ideology altogether, one associated with the world view of shamanism.

Shamanism is a widespread and apparently very ancient pattern of beliefs and activities. According to Åke Hultkrantz, whose training and work combine the fields of anthropology and history of religions, shamanism is not a religion, but a "religious configuration" or "complex." It is "a semi-independent segment of an ethnic religion," a "nuclear feature" of which is "a belief system . . . an ideology and a set of expectations concerning shamans" (1978, 29). This complex has several "important constituents." For one, shamanism is based on a particular "ideological premise," namely a cosmology that postulates a supernatural world and means of communication with it. In addition, members of their societies share certain beliefs about shamans: that they are intermediaries "between the human group and the supernaturals," that they receive inspiration from their "guardian or helping spirits," and that they have "ecstatic experiences." In their role as intermediaries, shamans can have a variety of functions—curing, divination, charming game animals, and the like—but they are usually not in charge of the cult (30–48).[13]

Accounting for resuscitation. In the Hebrew Bible, stories of the dead brought back to life are unique to the Elijah and Elisha narratives.

Elsewhere in the Hebrew Bible, there is no reticence about attributing to Yahweh mighty acts in the world of human experience, but resuscitation was apparently not considered to be part of Yahweh's repertoire. Therefore, the first and most obvious tension between these stories and the Deuteronomic ideology arises from the need to account for the very idea that resuscitation was a live possibility. The narratives leave us in the dark about what Elijah and Elisha thought they were doing in the ritual itself. Apparently, they had some hopes of reviving their patients, but how did they and those who called upon them understand what they hoped would take place?

Our approach to this problem begins with the observation that though the two stories in Kings differ in length and in some details, they are remarkably similar in both structure and content. The narratives display a definite pattern with the following elements: (1) introduction (1 Kgs. 17:8–16—this account of how the prophet came to take up residence in Zarephath in the house of a widow provides the introduction to the Elijah story; 2 Kgs. 4:8–17); (2) the illness is reported (17:17; 4:20); (3) help is sought from the prophet (17:18–19a; 4:21–28); (4) the prophet performs a healing ritual (17:19b–21; 4:29–35); (5) the ritual's success is reported (17:22–23; 4:36); and (6) a response to the cure occurs (17:24; 4:37). Furthermore, the healing rituals themselves are identical in structure: The patient is laid out on a bed in the prophet's chamber (17:19, 4:21); when he is alone with the corpse, the prophet cries out (prays) to Yahweh (17:20; 4:33), then mounts the bed and lays himself upon the body (Elijah does this three times, Elisha twice; 17:21, 4:34–35).

It is striking that this pattern of ritual activity has close parallels in ethnographic reports of shamanic curing among tribal peoples. In one account, a Northern Ojibwa shaman was summoned to cure a sick girl, but she died soon after his arrival. At once the shaman "tied a piece of red yarn around the girl's wrist," laid her body out, and lay down beside her. He lay very still, then after a while "began to move ever so little. The girl began to move a little also . . . [he] moved a little more. So did the girl. Finally . . . [he] raised himself into a sitting posture and at the same time the girl" did likewise (Hallowell 1967, 154–55).

In this case a native explanation of the dynamics of resuscitation is available. From the Ojibwa point of view, the doctor had followed the girl's soul to the land of the dead, captured it, and brought it back before its residence there became permanent. The red yarn tied around the patient's wrist was to make his task of identifying the proper soul easier. A. I. Hallowell assures us that according to the Northern Ojibwa "theory of the nature of things" such feats were possible, though only the most powerful doctors could perform them (1967, 154)[14]

Another parallel to the Elijah and Elisha narratives comes from southeastern Siberia (Lopatin 1946–49). In this case the patient was a young boy, and although he was not dead, the healing ritual displays the pattern I have been discussing. The shaman sat at the boy's bedside "singing a plaintive, monotonous song" that first emphasized how poor and defenseless the boy's family and he himself were and then went on to extol the power of his spirit protector ("All the spirits tremble before my master. . . . Certainly he will help us."). To the accompaniment of drums, the shaman danced around the fire, then stood beside the boy's bed and sang an invocation, expressing confidence that the spirit would come to help "these poor people." Again he danced around the fire, and then leapt to the front door, where he sang an invocation to his spirit protector. Suddenly the shaman shuddered and stopped singing. In a changed voice that signaled the coming of the spirit, he shouted, "I am here; I have come to help these poor people. I will look at the child." "In a state of ecstasy," he approached the boy's bed and "crouched over him" until their faces almost touched. He then ran around the room beating his drum crying out, "I am flying. . . . I will catch you." From time to time he spoke in different voices, apparently representing a dialogue between spirits, and finally he cried, "I have it; I have it!," cupping his hands "as though he held something in them." At this point the parents rushed to the bed and pulled the blanket off the boy. The shaman jumped in beside him, and the parents covered them both with the blanket. "After a few minutes," the shaman got out and began again to dance and sing. When he was completely exhausted, the parents placed him on a bed opposite the boy's, and he slept (365–67).

Speaking later with the researcher, Ivan Lopatin, the shaman "explained that the boy was sick because his soul had been stolen by a spirit." The running and leaping around the room represented the shaman's flight "into the spirit realm," where he found the offending spirit and recaptured the boy's soul and brought it back "in the shape of a sparrow." Lopatin confessed that he had not seen this sparrow, but both his interpreter and the boy's parents assured him that they had seen it quite plainly. The shaman also said "that while lying beside the boy he had restored the soul to the body" (367–68). These are not isolated examples, either in the idea that the dead can be revived, or in the particular form that the therapeutic act takes, or in the understanding that the cause of the illness was soul loss.

We might inquire about the sense of the term *dead* in such reports. The usual assumption by researchers is that the patient is unconscious, perhaps near death, but that death in the medical or biological sense had not yet occurred. Speaking of Paviotso (Northern Paiute) shamanism, R. H. Lowie says, "When a person 'died,' i.e., was very sick, the shaman would lie beside him and also 'die' for several hours in order to bring him back" (1924, 294). A similar understanding is reflected in native ideas that if the procedure is to be successful, the person cannot have been "dead" too long. Thus, one of Willard Z. Park's Northern Paiute informants, Rosie Plummer, said, "When someone dies suddenly, there is time to get a shaman. If the soul has not gone far, he can bring it back. He goes into a trance to bring back the soul. When the soul has gone a long way to the afterworld, the shaman cannot do anything. It has too much of a start to the land of the dead and he cannot overtake it" (1938, 41; cf. Whiting 1950, 40–42). Too much time cannot have elapsed (cf. Haeberlin 1918, 249–50), and signs of decomposition of the corpse signal that "death [in the medical sense] has really occurred" (Shirokogoroff 1935, 320). Sometimes a person is considered dead when some of the vital signs are still present. The Washo believe that "soul loss may result in death. . . . 'A person's spirit leaves him before he passes out. He is still breathing but he is really dead.' It is possible, however, to recapture the soul, to bring it back to its former physical vesture. The shaman, who knows when the soul has taken flight, will dispatch his power and commission it to fetch back the departed 'life.'" Furthermore, shamans in trance "are counted dead" (Siskin 1983, 52).[15]

The Elisha account does not clearly explain the boy's coming back to life, saying only that his body warmed and then he winked (or sneezed) and opened his eyes (4:34–35). The Elijah story, however, links the resuscitation to the return of the *nepeš* ("soul" or "breath"): the prophet called upon Yahweh to let the boy's *nepeš* return to his "inward parts"; Yahweh listened, the *nepeš* returned, and the boy lived (17:21–22). The similarity in physical activities, together with the native explanations of resuscitation and healing we have just examined, suggest the possibility that the Elijah (and by inference the Elisha) narrative assumes a soul-loss theory of illness and death.

This idea seems to go against a consensus among biblical scholars that the Old Testament conception of *nepeš* is distinctly different from the dualistic conception we encounter in Greek philosophy and Gnosticism. According to L. R. Bailey, "in traditional biblical thought, death was total (there is no distinction between body and soul)." The Greeks, however, "introduced a new view of humans," namely, the notion of a soul that was "detachable from the corpse" (1985, 213). Thus, Roland de Vaux claims that "the distinction between soul and body is something foreign to the Hebrew mentality, and death, therefore, is not regarded as the separation of these two elements" (1961, 56; cf. Porteous 1962, 428). Genesis 2:7 is often considered a key text in this discussion. Michael Knibb says this verse "epitomises the Old Testament view of the constitution of man." In this view there is no dichotomy between body and soul: "the 'breath of life' is not conceived of as having an existence somehow separate from the body, and it is man as an entity who becomes a 'living being'" (1989, 398). The individual human being is understood to be "a centre of consciousness and unit of vital power" (Johnson 1964, 19).

But matters do not appear to be that simple. The word *nepeš* has many connotations, running from physical (throat, neck, breath, body, blood) and emotional (hunger, thirst, grieving, desire, agreement) associations to "life" in the abstract and even "corpse" (Num. 19:11–33; cf. Johnson 1964, 3–22, Brotzman 1988). It is especially important to note that *nepeš* can be distinguished from "flesh" (*bāśār*; Deut. 12:23, Isa. 10:18), and that it departs from the dying person (Gen. 35:18; the same idea, but using the term *rûaḥ*, "spirit," appears in Pss. 104:29, 146:4; Job 34:14–5; Eccles. 12:7). The *nepeš* is said to be poured out when one is sick (Job 30:16) or starving (Lam. 2:12). Recovery from illness can be described as Yahweh bringing up the *nepeš* from Sheol (the underworld; Ps. 30:2–3). The term *rûaḥ* ("spirit", "wind") has a similar range of connotations (Johnson 1964, 23–37).

Furthermore, the Hebrew Bible contains clear evidence that at least some Israelites believed that some aspect of an individual could survive the death of the physical body. One finds, for example, references to grave offerings (Deut. 26:14, Sir. 30:18) and to diviners who employed "ghosts" and "familiar spirits" (Lev. 19:31; 20:6, 27; Deut. 18:11; Isa. 8:19, 19:3). Saul's consultation at Endor with "a woman who is *master* of a ghost" (*'ēšeh ba'ălat-'ôb*; 1 Sam. 28:7) is particularly striking, since she divined by the "ghost" of a known historical figure, Samuel. Some thought that disembodied spirits (*rĕpā'îm*, "shades") resided in Sheol (Job 26:5, Isa. 14:9–10; cf. Ezek. 32:21).[16]

Although scholars have been attentive to the apparent contrast between Hebrew and Hellenistic conceptions of soul and body, they have generally failed to be sufficiently sensitive to the folk background of ancient Israelite culture. The evidence just cited suggests that at least some persons in the society in which the Elijah and Elisha narratives were produced would have been prepared to believe that sickness and death were the result of the loss of the soul and that curing these conditions involved recovering the errant soul and reintroducing it into the body. Such a notion lies outside the Deuteronomic ideology of the narratives. It does, however, offer an explanation of our first tension.[17]

Blaming the Prophets; Blaming Yahweh. The second and third tensions between the Deuteronomic ideology and the characterization of Elijah and Elisha form a pair and may be dealt with together. In the stories it appears the prophets are held responsible for the boys' deaths. Thus, the mother confronts Elijah with an accusation that he has caused the death of her son (1 Kgs. 17:18), while Elisha is accused of deceit (2 Kgs. 4:28; cf. 4:16). There are other texts, of course, where prophets are treated as adversaries, but in these other texts the dispute lies in the political (Jer. 26:7–11) or the theological-political (Jer. 28:1–11, 29:24–8) spheres. The mothers' accusations are, by contrast, quite personal in nature.[18] For their part, the prophets pass the blame on to Yahweh. Elijah's rhetorical question has the effect of explicitly accusing Yahweh of killing the boy (1 Kgs. 17:20), and Elisha's comment to Gehazi ("she is in bitter distress; Yahweh has hidden it from me and has not told me," 2 Kgs. 4:27) hints at a similar sentiment. At the very least, Elisha is accusing Yahweh of withholding vital information from him.

Among the common characteristics of the relatively diverse and fluid religious phenomenon known as shamanism are the putative power of shamans "to control the spirits, usually by incarnating them," and "to engage in mystical flight and other 'out of body experiences'" (I. M. Lewis 1986, 88). Shamans were recognized as powerful individuals whose role was to uphold the welfare of the local community. The way of conceiving the shaman's defense of the community differs, of course, from group to group. A. Anisimov provides a particularly striking account of a Siberian cosmology in which the shaman's task is to set spirit guards around the perimeter of the clan's territory to ward off hostile spirits that might enter and create havoc, as well as to cure those who have fallen victim to such an attack (cf. Overholt 1986, 158–65). When disaster strikes, people might blame the shaman, who might in turn accuse a spirit familiar.[19]

Protection may take other forms. Among the Korekore of Zimbabwe, traditional holy men, referred to in the literature as spirit mediums, are associated with specific territories, or "land-shrine neighborhoods." The spirit-guardians of these neighborhoods "are exhorted to bring the rain and make the crops grow" (Garbett 1969, 120). The well-being of the community is thought to be dependent upon everyone coming together in amity for certain rituals, and during these the spirit medium becomes possessed and, "speaking as the spirit-guardian," urges the people to uphold traditional norms and refrain from activities (like sorcery, incest, adultery, and homicide) that may anger the spirit-guardian and (in the case of homicide) pollute the land as well. Mediums are also called on to mediate disputes between members of the community.

They are thus "important in the maintenance of community values at the local level" (120–21), and since the "Korekore believe that a disturbance in the moral order produces disturbances in the natural order" (125), this protection of the community has a cosmic dimension. It may be possible to see here a parallel to Elisha's involvement in the new moon and sabbath celebrations referred to by the Shunemite woman's husband (2 Kgs. 4:23), particularly if these were concerned with the fertility of the land.[20]

The Korekore spirit mediums also help maintain political stability by resolving disputes over succession to chief (1966, 152–55). This calls to mind the involvement of Elijah and Elisha in determining succession to the Israelite throne (cf. 1 Kgs. 19:16, 2 Kgs. 9:1–13).[21]

It is worth noting that the resuscitation stories depict Elijah and Elisha as familiar figures who are known to be capable of powerful acts. In Elijah's case circumstances limit the scope of this recognition. On the run from the Israelite king and hiding in territory controlled by Sidon, his reputation is nevertheless established in the mind of the widow in whose house he had taken refuge by the previous episode of multiplying her meager supply of oil and flour (17:8–16). In the case of Elisha, the narrative suggests that he made regular rounds and performed specific functions on the people's behalf (4:8–10, 23).

These stories do not specifically claim that Elijah and Elisha controlled the deity who effected the resuscitations (acceptance of the Deuteronomic ideology of the narratives renders such an idea unthinkable), but the diviner of Endor's "mastery" of Samuel's ghost suggests there may have been some for whom that would have been the "natural" explanation. And if their patrons believed these prophets to have such powers, it would have been natural to blame the arrival of misfortune on the prophets' lack of diligence, their duplicity, or the like.

It is not unusual for members of a group to have an ambivalent attitude toward their shaman. Edgar Siskin, for example, found that negative feelings about shamans were an important factor in the acceptance of the new peyote religion among some Washo Indians (western Nevada) in the late 1930s. Shamans could cure, but they could also be sorcerers. "Fear and hatred of the shaman" were part of traditional Washo culture, and in the old days there were ways of resolving this—shamans who used sorcery to murder others were themselves killed.[22] In the 1930s this solution was no longer available, and peyote provided "an opportunity to defy and challenge the shamans" and deprive them of financial support and prestige (Siskin 1983, 144–46). The shaman "is an ambiguous or liminal figure. . . . He is neither inherently good nor evil, because he works for the benefit, as well as for the misfortune, of others" (Langdon 1992a, 12). Elisha proved himself something of a danger-ous sorcerer by sending disease on his servant Gehazi (2 Kgs.5:26–7), not to mention the bizarre story about his causing the death of forty-two "small boys" (2 Kgs. 4:23–25). Rofé speaks of the "ambivalent presenta-tion of the character of Elisha" in 2 Kings 6:24–7:20—he is both a "sor-cerer possessing supernatural powers, who sees and hears from afar (6:32), and who by himself brings down curses upon his enemies with-out God's intervention (7:1, 19–20)" and a prophet who speaks in the name of Yahweh (1988, 70; cf. 16). And it is possible that 2 Kings 1:2–8 reflects a similar fear of Elijah on the part of Ahaziah. This may help explain the widow's suggestion that Elijah was responsible for the death of her son (1 Kgs. 17:18) and the combativeness of the Shunemite woman when she sought Elisha's aid (2 Kgs. 4:28, 30).

These tensions, then, turn out to be very great. The shamanic world view presupposes the existence of multiple powerful spirits that can potentially be pressed into service by powerful humans. Such a view is submerged by the ideology of the resuscitation narratives in Kings. But it is well to remember that in the narratives of 1 Kings 17–2 Kings 13 Yahweh is not the sole spirit inhabitant of even Yahweh's own heaven (1 Kgs. 22:19–23), and that Yahweh's supremacy is not assured, but a mat-ter of dispute (1 Kgs. 18:21, 2 Kgs. 1:2–4).

The prophet as healer. The fourth point of tension is implicit in the first three. The resuscitation narratives assume that prophets are able to help in cases of serious illness (cf. also 2 Kgs. 5:3), and that one may seek them out for help with essentially personal problems rather than the problems of the nation. So it is with shamans, who are mainly heal-ers, the doctors and protectors of their local residence groupings. When one is ill, these are the professionals to whom one turns.

Curing is everywhere the (or one of the) principal job(s) of the shaman. In a recent study of health and medicine in Native North Amer-ican cultures, Åke Hultkrantz stresses "that Native American medical beliefs and practices can be assessed only in relation to their religious ideas. Health, disease, and death are woven into a pattern that is under-standable only if we see it from the point of view of religion. . . . Native American healers have paid their greatest attention to a psychosomatic medicine that is directly related to religion—a medicinal dimension largely absent among Western doctors" (1992, xv; at least, one might add, until relatively recently). Although "true" shamanism is associated with hunting and gathering cultures, Hultkrantz argues that all Native American curing has a "shamanic substructure," which in Pueblo and other horticultural societies may be "transformed into sacerdotal ritual-ism" (158–62).

It is easy to find evidence in North America and elsewhere of the importance of curing. Willard Park is unequivocal: "Curing is the chief function of the Paviotso shaman" (1938, 45), and this function is stressed in virtually all the studies in a recent collection on Native South American shamanism (Langdon and Baer 1992). Haeberlin tells us that among the coast Salish (Puget Sound) there are a number of different "shamanistic guardian-spirits . . . but they all refer to the power of healing" (1918, 250). Siberian shamans enlist the aid of their spirit-helpers in combating disease (Anisimov 1963, in Overholt 1986, 150–58; cf. Mikhailovskii 1895, 90–95, 97–100, 126–28, 142–43; Shirokogoroff 1935, 313 and often). Raymond Firth says that "the most important social function [of African spirit mediums] is to provide treatment for sick people" (1969, xiii). The same seems true for shamans among the Hill Saora of Orissa, India (Elwin 1955, in Overholt 1986, 268–72).

Rofé has recognized this connection. In the context of discussing possible modern analogies to the main character in the prophetic *legenda*, "a local figure whose miracles benefited a small group of admirers," he suggests that we ask where in contemporary society the functions performed by such a person take place. The functions turn out to be "mainly 'minor miracles,' performed in matters of sickness and health. . . . In modern society these tasks are performed by doctors, and just as the Man of God replaced the primitive medicine man, he himself was eventually replaced by the modern medical doctor" (1988, 20–21). Rofé's analogy is apt insofar as it focuses on the role of the "man of God" as healer, but we should beware of the implicit assumption of something like an evolutionary development from shaman to Elijah and Elisha to modern physicians. For we have seen (and will see more) evidence suggesting that the narratives picture Elijah and Elisha acting *like* shamans.

It is often difficult to separate strictly the two main shamanic functions of protecting the community and curing illness. The Evenks, a Tungus people of western Siberia, assume "that spirits of disease and death were sent to people by shamans alien to the clan." To protect against these, clan shamans constructed a "mythical shamanistic fence [*marylya*] or stockade made out of spirits." Curing performances are elaborate battles against these outside forces (Anisimov 1963, 107, 111, 113; cf. Overholt 1986, 150–65). "From the point of view of shamanistic ideology, the fate of the clan was wholly in the shaman's hands" (113). To cite one more example, the *mabolong* ritual of the Wana (Indonesia) is a community affair involving several shamans, who enlist the aid of their "spirit familiars" to diagnose and cure patients. The dramatic effect is an identification of the audience with the shaman, an identification that overcomes the centrifugal tendencies of society. "In ritual and in everyday life, this is the accomplishment of a successful shaman: ritually, he overcomes the dissolution of his patients' beings; socially, he attracts and maintains a following of neighbors whose commitment to and dependence on him lends stability to a community" (Atkinson 1987, 351). All of this describes a conceptual world in which, in general, the stories about Elija and Elisha are at home.

Thus a subtext in the Elijah and Elisha narratives reveals an understanding of the relationships between humans and deity that contrasts with more familiar biblical representations of Yahweh and Yahweh's people. The presence of this subtext is betrayed by four points at which the Elijah and Elisha resuscitation narratives stand in tension with the Deuteronomic history's construction of reality. These tensions suggest that implicit in these stories is a code—a set of rules about how Israelite prophets acted, at least in some circumstances—associated with the world view of shamanism.[23] This code forms part of the "determinative substantive content" of the texts, and if we do not recognize this aspect of their author's (or authors') mindset, we will miss an important dimension of the text's meaning, as well as clues to the life-experience out of which it arose.[24]

This interpretation of the resuscitation stories does not solve standard literary and form-critical problems, but attempts to gain some insight into difficult aspects of the texts that these methods are not well equipped to address. It does raise historical problems, however, since it suggests that the Elijah and Elisha narratives as we have them simultaneously reflect two somewhat different ideologies. To attempt to trace the origins of either ideology in ancient Israel would be a highly speculative undertaking. From a global perspective, the shamanic world view is older than the Yahwistic by millennia. Since the development of societies is not characterized by any neat evolution from earlier (and more "primitive") to later forms, however, we may conclude that the contestatory nature of the narratives indicates that both views were operative in Ahab's Israel. Over time aspects of Israelite religion such as those we have discovered in these prophetic stories were no doubt contested and changed through processes familiar to all students of culture. It is entirely reasonable that prophets like Elijah and Elisha were a part of that process.

To speak of this kind of cultural change raises another issue. At least since the time of E. B. Tylor, some anthropologists have used the term *survivals*, to refer to "functionless crude or superstitious elements of belief or custom [which can] be found in civilized societies." These are considered "to be the fossilized remains" (analogous to the *k* in the word *knight*, which is "functionless in speech") of things that in earlier times were characteristic of the whole society. This notion of survivals tends to be tied to evolutionistic assumptions about progress and stages of development through which all societies are believed to pass. It has been criticized by diffusionists for taking things out of context and ignoring historical processes and evidence (Rogerson 1978, 23–24, 32–35).

Shamanism is without doubt a more ancient religious pattern than priestly religion, and thus it seems to make sense to think of resuscitations as survivals, that is, as beliefs and practices that appear not to have been current in monarchic Israel and that seem to make connection with beliefs and practices prevalent in different (and in some respects less developed) cultural settings.[25] On the other hand, the evidence shows that these "resuscitations" are part of a shamanistic pattern that was an integral and functioning part (how widespread or important a part is another question) of society during the Israelite monarchy.

The way out of this dilemma lies in I. M. Lewis's more nuanced conception of the nature of survivals. Lewis notes the presence in North African Islam of phenomena—such as the veneration of saints, possession cults, and brotherhoods—that from one point of view appear to have their roots in pre-Islamic beliefs and practices. Viewed in context, however, they have become important parts of the practice of Islam in this region (1986, 94–107). This is the way we should view the shamanistic pattern discernible in the Elijah and Elisha narratives. It is not a remnant of some "pure" and exotic Siberian shamanism, on its last legs in Israel and about to disappear in the evolutionary triumph of a higher religious form, monotheism. It is rather a pattern heavily influenced by Yahwism and part of it. Elements of this pattern can be discerned in biblical accounts of prophecy in Israel, and its presence endures in the Jewish and Christian religious traditions (cf. Overholt 1989).

Finally, it is remarkable that the Hebrew Bible's most detailed accounts of cures reflect this shamanistic background. Apparently, none of the mainstream versions of Yahwism, at least so far as we know them, had any positive interest in curing as a religious activity. This is no doubt a reflection of the structure of, and tensions within, Israelite society, matters we will turn to shortly.

"Miracles" and Belief

Many of the episodes in the Elijah and Elisha narratives refer to unusual occurrences, acts of power that, because they fall outside normal expectations about what humans can accomplish, might be referred to as miracles.[26] Thus in addition to causing (2 Kgs. 5:26–27) and curing (the resuscitations) disease, these "men of God" multiply meager supplies of food (1 Kgs. 17:13–16; 2 Kgs. 4:1–7, 42–44), call down fire from heaven (1 Kgs. 18:36–38, 2 Kgs. 1:9–12), part the waters of the Jordan (2 Kgs. 2:8, 14), purify poisonous food (2 Kgs. 2:21, 4:40–41), command wild animals (2 Kgs. 2:24), cause iron to float (2 Kgs. 6:6), and first afflict with blindness, then cure, a whole army (2 Kgs. 6:15–20). In this feature we have another potential tie to the conceptual world of shamanism.

It is not necessary to assume a historical kernel behind any of these accounts. In fact, we have already noted that some take up traditional folklore themes (the inexhaustible food supply) and that in the context of shamanistic curing, "death" is not necessarily equated with the cessation of biological functions. Such stories may, however, reveal something about the motives of the people who told them, and it is possible to generalize about the social function of miracles in the context of shamanism: They serve to legitimate and enhance the authority of the persons about whom they are told. The story of Elijah's contest with the Baal prophets on Mount Carmel makes this explicit. After preparing his offering, Elijah prayed, "O Yahweh . . . let it be known this day that you are God in Israel, that I am your servant, and that I have done all these things at your bidding" (1 Kgs. 18:36). When the fire fell from heaven and consumed the offering, "the people saw it [and] . . . fell on their faces and said, 'Yahweh indeed is God, Yahweh indeed is God.'" (1 Kgs. 18–39)[27] The same motivation seems to be behind Elisha's message to the king of Israel, who was distressed when Naaman the Syrian came to him seeking a cure for his leprosy: "'Why have you torn your clothes? Let him come to me, that he may learn that there is a prophet in Israel'" (2 Kgs. 5:8).

Such acts of power, sometimes referred to in anthropological literature as "tricks," are often part of shamanic performances. Some Paiute shamans are said to have walked on hot coals, to have put hot coals or a hot knife or a burning bundle of reeds into their mouths, and to have demonstrated their invulnerability to bullets fired from guns (Park 1938, 57–60; Whiting 1950, 40). Park says of such performances, "the singing and the shaman's tricks appear to have excited the spectators to a high emotional pitch which was followed by a relaxation of tension attended often by a general feeling of satisfaction when control of the sickness was demonstrated by the return of the soul or the extraction of a disease-object" (47). Mikhailovskii (1895) mentions a variety of tricks in the repertoire of Siberian and European Russian shamans, including cutting the tongue until blood flows (68); stabbing oneself in the stomach (69, 136); being shot with arrow or bullet (134, 137); immunity to fire (134); swallowing sticks, hot coals, or glass (137); decapitation (137, 140); displaying supernormal physical power (137); and Houdini-like escapes from bondage (137). The last of these was a standard feature of Plains Indian Yuwipi ceremonies. The shaman was wrapped in a quilt and bound with rawhide cords and the lights extinguished. There followed visual and auditory indications of the presence of spirits (flying objects brushing against the participants, sparks, thumps, and the like), and when the light was turned on the shaman would be sitting with the quilt neatly folded and the cord rolled into a ball (see Overholt 1986, 77–86).

In the shaking tent ceremony found among Indians of the northern Woodlands, the shaman would enter a specially constructed cylindrical structure and summon spirits who could be consulted by those in attendance concerning such problems as the location of lost or stolen objects. Some of these shamans (they are often referred to in the literature as "conjurers") were said to be capable of impressive tricks, such as tossing lost articles out of the tent. According to Hallowell, who studied the Northern Ojibwa version of this ceremony, these tricks "enhance their personal reputations and probably support the native theory of conjuring even in the minds of other conjurers who are unable to duplicate them, although they may have tricks of their own." He goes on to say that "the respect, if not awe, which the demonstration of unique powers meets, is ample motivation for the individual who craves prestige. It is perhaps the major type of social recognition which this society has to offer. But it can only be won and maintained by actual demonstrations of magic power in competition with others" (1942, 71, 72; cf. 68–72). Similarly, after describing a variety of "tricks" (the people are bilingual, and this is the term they now use) employed by shamans on St. Lawrence Island (Bering Sea, Alaska)—among them gnawing one's hands bloody and then healing them by licking, making parkas levitate, and producing sounds of spirits walking around underneath the floor—Jane Murphy says, "Whatever the specific content of this part of the performance, the common purpose was the spectacular establishment of the preternatural powers of the chief actor in the drama before his audience (1964, 59–60)."[28]

A similar dynamic connected with the acts of power in the Elijah and Elisha narratives is indicated by the nature of the responses the stories incorporate. The widow whose son Elijah has resuscitated says, "Now I know that you are a man of God, and that the word of Yahweh in your mouth is truth" (1 Kgs. 17:24). The army captain, like his predecessors faced with immolation, acknowledges Elijah's power and begs to be spared (2 Kgs. 1:13–14). The sons of the prophets, having witnessed Elisha splitting the waters of the Jordan, are said to have exclaimed, "The spirit of Elijah rests on Elisha" (2 Kgs. 2:15), and the Shunemite woman whose son had been restored to life "came and fell at (Elisha's) feet, bowing to the ground" (2 Kgs. 4:37). Naaman, cured of his leprosy, acknowledges Yahweh's power and, implicitly, that of Elisha (2 Kgs. 5:15–19). I have already called attention to the response of the people on Mount Carmel.

Rofé makes a similar point with respect to the short *legenda* (for example, 2 Kgs. 4:1–7, 38–41, 42–44), which he views as "popular tales" about local figures whose "miracles are minor deliverances" that "lack national or theological significance" and are "deficient in moral values." The "feeling of fear and respect towards the Man of God" demanded of the characters in these stories "hints at . . . their unconscious message. These tales express the attitude of fear and admiration of the simple believer towards the Holy Man, his wonder at the supernatural acts of the Man of God and his excitement at the involvement of the Divine in daily affairs" (1988, 13–16).

Other avenues of interpretation exist, of course. In 1935 Albrecht Alt proposed a theory, since widely accepted, that a historical occurrence— the reannexation by Israel of a border territory lost during the reign of Solomon—lies behind the legendary account of the contest on Mount Carmel. Against such historicizing interpretations Ernst Würthwein argues that the narrative's account of a miracle identifies it as a "religious-mythic statement shaped by faith" (1989, 280). 1 Kings 18:21–39 has no historical kernel. To the contrary, it is "a piece of [Deuteronomistic] narrative theology" growing out of a "monotheistic faith" that insists on worshipping the incomparable God, Yahweh, and condemns worship of Baal as senseless (283).

The general principle at work in Würthwein's interpretation is that the presence of miracles should warn us against looking for history and should cause us to focus on the author's "intended kerygma" (284). Thus, as a matter of strategy, when they encounter miracle stories some interpreters look for an underlying historical event, others for kerygma. But we may look elsewhere—to parallels from anthropology—and consider the social, rather than the theological, function of such "tricks." It is significant that virtually all of the miraculous actions attributed to prophets in the Hebrew Bible occur in the Elijah and Elisha narratives.[29] The fit is with the conceptual world of shamanism.

Knowledge of Things Far Off

We are accustomed to associate prophecy with prediction, which in the Bible is understood to be based on the prophet's knowledge of God's intention. Such predictions may be found in the Elijah and Elisha narratives. Indeed, the cycle begins with one: "As Yahweh the God of Israel lives, before whom I stand, there shall be neither dew nor rain these years, except by my word" (1 Kgs. 17:1; other examples include 21:19 and 2 Kgs. 3:16–9).

In several episodes, however, Elisha is said to have a somewhat different kind of nonordinary knowledge: knowledge of things currently taking place elsewhere. In the story of Naaman's cure, Elisha refused payment, but his servant, Gehazi, acted secretly in order to enrich himself. Although he was not present, Elisha knew what Gehazi had done and confronted him: "Did I not go with you in spirit when someone left his chariot to meet you? Is this a time to accept money and to accept clothing, olive orchards and vineyards, sheep and oxen, male and female slaves?" (2 Kgs. 5:26, NRSV; Hebrew: "did my heart not go . . . "). Elisha is also said to have known the battle plans of the king of Aram (6:8–12), and to have been aware "before the messenger arrived" that the king of Israel had dispatched an emissary to take him into custody (6:32).

Shamans are also said to know things that are happening far away or are otherwise hidden from ordinary human perception. Hallowell tells us that the Ojibwa shaking tent "conjurer is a specialist in invocation. The most characteristic function which he exercises through the aid of his spiritual helpers is seership or clairvoyance" (1942, 9; cf. Jenness 1935, 63–65). Aided by the spirit-helpers he summons, the conjurer is able to learn about far-off people or events and find "lost or stolen articles," as well as predict the future, diagnose the cause of sickness, abduct souls, and find game (Hallowell 1942, 12, 53–72). Hallowell attended a ceremony at which three pieces of information supplied by the spirits about the condition of absent persons proved subsequently to be true (46–47). He also cites a report of an eighteenth-century conjuring ceremony held at Sault Ste. Marie and witnessed by the trader Alexander Henry. The local Ojibwa were uncertain whether to attend a conference to which they had been invited by Sir William Johnson because they feared a trap. A conjurer "journeyed all the way to Fort Niagara and Montreal and after 'a quarter of an hour elapsed in silence' he returned and 'delivered a lengthy speech,'" the gist of which was that it was safe and many presents would be offered. The group decided to go (1942, 65–66). These reports reflect two sources of the shaman's special knowledge: spirit-helpers, who seek out and report the desired information, and the shaman's own soul, which travels abroad to obtain it.

The case is the same in the closely related shaking tent rite of the Plains Blackfoot[30] and the Yuwipi ceremony of the Lakota (Sioux). Yuwipi men are noted for their ability to determine the location of lost or stolen objects and missing persons (Overholt 1986, 79; Lame Deer 1972, 187; Powers, 1977, 146–47). Lame Deer, himself a Yuwipi man, explains that wrapped and bound in his blanket the shaman "is now as one who is dead . . . his spirit could be hundreds of miles away in the far hills, conversing with the ancient ones." At the end of the ceremony, people may ask questions, and the Yuwipi man will answer. "If he is good, if he has the power, he already has been told the answers while he was lying in the dark inside the blanket" (Lame Deer 1972, 194–6).

Such ideas are widespread. Tlingit Indians of the Northwest Coast believed that shamans could send out their spirits to gather information (Hultkrantz 1992, 61), and Shirokogoroff tells of a female shaman of the Khingan Tungus who went in ecstasy "to the wigwam of the family" of the client, which was sixty miles away, and on her return "reported how the members of the family were doing" (1935, 312; cf. 361). Again, a peculiar element in the Elijah and Elisha narratives proves susceptible of interpretation in the context of the conceptual world of shamanism.

Paraphernalia and Assistants

A unique feature in the Elisha story is the proxy action involving Gehazi and Elisha's staff (2 Kgs. 4:29–31). The narrator does not make Elisha's motivation clear, but we may find a clue to what is going on in reports that shamans sometimes had staffs as part of their paraphernalia and employed them in curing. Lowie tells of a Paiute shaman, Coffee Charlie, who doctored a boy "who had been given up by the white physician." He used a specially decorated "stick about four feet long," which he "set at the patient's head." Coffee Charlie "went into a trance, then the boy was placed on him so that the pits of their stomachs were together." The shaman "shook his rattle; at first the sound seemed far away, but gradually it got closer and closer. The boy at first did not recognize his mother, but did a little later. He recovered" (1924, 294; cf. Park 1938, 34, 56, 134). Staffs were also part of the paraphernalia of some Siberian shamans (Shirokogoroff 1935, 290; Hajdú 1968) and Zimbabwean spirit mediums (Garbett 1969, 116). The urgency of Gehazi's errand (v. 29) can be explained by the idea that resuscitation cannot succeed if the patient has been "dead" for too long.[31]

If the staff is unique in these stories, the figure of Gehazi is not. Elijah had a servant ("young man," *na'ar*; 1 Kgs. 18:43, 19:3) who predates the anointing of Elisha, who is himself once referred to as Elijah's "attendant" (1 Kgs. 19:21). Elisha may have had several servants. Gehazi is mentioned by name (2 Kgs. 4:12, 25; 5:20; 8:4), and there are several anonymous figures (2 Kgs. 5:22; 6:15, 17; see 4:43, where a different term is used), including "the young man, the servant of the prophet" (2 Kgs. 9:4)[32] who was sent to anoint Jehu. The stories indicate that such persons are sometimes given tasks by their master.

This is another feature shared with shamanism. Paiute shamans sometimes had assistants who helped them during the course of curing ceremonies (Whiting 1950, 41–42; Park 1938, 54), and the same is true of Tungus shamans in Siberia (Anisimov 1963, in Overholt 1986, 153–54). The necessity for an assistant is particularly acute in these instances, since certain tasks must be performed while the shaman is in a state of trance. We will return to the matter of prophetic ecstasy in the next section.

ELIJAH AND ELISHA IN ISRAELITE SOCIETY

Up to this point we have examined specific features of the Elijah and Elisha narratives that data from anthropological field studies can help us understand: folkloristic elements in the stories, curing, resuscitation, miracles, knowledge-at-a-distance, and the shaman's paraphernalia and assistants. Comparative data support the conclusion that the conceptual horizon of these features is to be found in a shamanic world view. In the Hebrew Bible, however, this cycle of stories is an integral part of a particular Yahwistic (the Deuteronomistic) interpretation of the history of Israel and Judah. In the stories as we have them in the books of Kings, this shamanistic tone is a subtext and not the sole point of view. Thus we now turn to anthropological theory for assistance in interpreting how these particular phenomena fit within the culture and society of monarchic Israel.

Elijah, Elisha, and the Symbols of Israelite Culture

In chapter 1 we examined the nature of society and culture. According to Clifford Geertz, culture is "an historically transmitted pattern of meanings embodied in symbols, a system of inherited conceptions . . . by means of which men communicate, perpetuate, and develop their knowledge about and attitudes toward life" (1973, 89). Since culture is public, we may gain "empirical access" to the symbol systems that embody and express it through observing the actions of its members (17). For the most part, anthropologists observe living people, though they may also (especially those who practice the subdiscipline of ethnohistory) make use of written material. Our access to Israelite behavior is much more restricted, being limited to ancient texts with some assistance from archaeology. Nevertheless, it is possible to discern several features of Israelite culture reflected in the narratives about Elijah and Elisha.

If, as I have suggested, one of the components of the culture of preexilic Israel is a pattern of meanings associated with shamanism, then what are the symbolic forms that embody this conception of reality? One possible answer is that we see reflected in the Elijah and Elisha narratives a symbol system with three interrelated components: the man of God, his acts of power, and characteristic possession behavior.

Man of God. "Man of God" is a title special to the Elijah and Elisha narratives. Nearly half the occurrences of the phrase in the Hebrew Bible are in these stories. The remainder are in Deuteronomic or post-Deuteronomic contexts, and David Petersen has argued that these are derivative from the prophetic legenda concerning Elijah and Elisha (1981, 40–43).

Elijah and Elisha are called "man of God" far more frequently (thirty-six times) than "prophet" (nine times), and the two terms occur together in only two of the twenty-five episodes of the cycle.[33] Furthermore, the contexts of the episodes in which these terms occur are, generally speaking, different. Where the term *prophet* occurs, Elijah and Elisha are pictured engaging in religious and/or political activity at the national level: the struggle with Ahab, Jezebel, and the Baal prophets (1 Kgs. 18:1–19:18),[34] the campaign in Moab (2 Kgs. 3:9–20), the defeat of the Aramaeans (2 Kgs. 6:8–23), and the anointing of Jehu (2 Kgs. 9:1–13). On the other hand, where they are called *man of God* the action is on a more local level: Elisha's interaction with the Shunemite woman (2 Kgs. 4:8–37) has nothing to do with the great issues of Yahweh versus Baal or succession to the throne.

Virtually all episodes containing the designation "man of God" are one of the types of legenda described by Rofé in his study of stories about prophets (1988). The extraordinary powers of the main character are a standard feature of such legenda, and all but one of the "man of God" episodes include the exercise of some remarkable power, like "miracles" or having knowledge of distant events (the exception is 2 Kgs. 13:14–19, a "normal" prophetic prediction). Those episodes that contain both titles combine actions of national significance with such acts of power (2 Kgs. 5:1–27, 6:8–23).

The narratives depict the relationship between Elijah and Elisha and the central government as at worst hostile and at best ambiguous. Elijah is on the whole antagonistic toward Ahab, whom he confronts on several occasions (1 Kgs. 17:1, 18:17–19, 21:17–24) and from whom he flees (1 Kgs. 17:2–24, 19:1–3), and toward Amaziah (2 Kgs. 1:2–17). Elisha sometimes seems to be on better terms with the king (2 Kgs. 4:13; 6:9,20–23; and by implication 8:1–6, 13:14–19), but other times not (2 Kings 6:31–32; note Elisha's involvement in Aramaean politics, 8:7–15, and his arranging the anointment of Jehu, who was to overthrow the dynasty of Ahab, 9:1). Given the overall tone of these stories, 2 Kings 5:8 is more likely to reflect competition between prophet and king than cooperation. Furthermore, though priesthood and sanctuaries existed in northern Israel, they play no part in the narratives. Elijah finds support among elements of the population who honor the "prophets of Yahweh" (Obadiah, 1 Kgs. 18:1–16), and the narratives suggest a close association of Elisha with "the sons of the prophets," a group or groups about which we know little.[35]

Petersen has argued that "man of God" denotes a specific role within Israelite society corresponding to the phenomenon I. M. Lewis calls peripheral possession (1981, 43–50).[36] In this analysis, referring to Elijah and Elisha as peripheral figures means not that they are outside of Israelite society, but that their position is secondary with respect to "the central institutions of the society" and that the people with whom they associate will tend to be "oppressed or underprivileged members of the society" (Petersen 1981, 44–45). If we take the monarchy and priestly religion to be the central institutions of Israelite society of the day, then the position of Elijah and Elisha does indeed seem to be peripheral.

The social status of their supporters is somewhat more ambiguous. Particularly the stories that mention the "sons of the prophets" reflect associations with persons who appear to be from the lower strata of society,[37] but this was not invariably the case. For example, Obadiah, a supporter of Elijah, is said to be an official in Ahab's palace (1 Kgs. 18:3), and the Shunemite woman is depicted as wealthy and in no need of political intervention (2 Kgs. 4:10–13). In the context of a shamanic pattern of assumptions and operation, this diversity is not a problem. The shaman responds to personal needs of all members of the group, not just those who are relatively disadvantaged.

In Lewis's analysis, other characteristics of peripheral possession are that it takes place in the context of a group that accepts and acknowledges the authority of the shaman, and that the god(s) of peripheral cults are themselves peripheral and tend to be amoral in their actions (cf. Petersen 1981, 45–46). Petersen cites references to the "sons of the prophets" as evidence of group support for the "holy man's" activity, and the apparent dominance of Baal worship during Ahab's reign as evidence that in a sense even Yahweh was peripheral to Israelite society. The capricious and destructive character of some of the powerful deeds recounted in these stories (for example, 1 Kgs. 18:38–40; 2 Kgs. 1:10, 12; 2:23–25) seems to confirm the amoral nature of Yahweh in this context (48–49).

Acts of power. The "miracles" that are a prominent feature of the Elijah and Elisha narratives have been treated above. It would be no exaggeration to say that these are a routine and expected part of the "man of God's" activity, and they trigger a predictable response.

Possession behavior. The questions of whether the prophets of the

Hebrew Bible had ecstatic experiences and, if they did, the nature of these experiences and of their relationship to the prophets' speech have been topics of scholarly debate for much of this century.[38] Regardless of the way we answer this question for the so-called writing prophets,[39] the Elijah and Elisha narratives contain evidence of possession behavior.

Consider, for example, the story of the war with Moab (2 Kgs. 3:4–27). Finding their campaign in jeopardy because of a lack of water, the kings of Israel, Judah, and Edom came to Elisha to "inquire of Yahweh." Elisha asked for a musician, and "while the musician was playing, the hand of Yahweh came on him. And he said, 'Thus says Yahweh . . . '" (vv. 15–16). How are we to interpret this close association of music, the "hand of Yahweh," and the prophetic oracle?

Although the phrase "hand of Yahweh" most often refers to Yahweh's power to effect historical or natural events,[40] it clearly designates some type of ecstatic experience in a number of passages, especially in Ezekiel. The imagery in Ezekiel 3:12–14 seems to combine behavior associated with the possession of a human individual by Yahweh's spirit with soul travel characteristic of a trance state: "Then the spirit lifted me up . . . .The spirit lifted me up and bore me away; I went in bitterness in the heat of my spirit, the hand of Yahweh being strong upon me."[41] Sometimes Ezekiel's being grasped by the hand of Yahweh is accompanied by hearing the deity speak.[42] At the conclusion of the Mount Carmel episode, this behavior takes the form of extraordinary physical activity: When the rain came, King Ahab rode off in his chariot. "But the hand of Yahweh was on Elijah; he girded up his loins and ran in front of Ahab to the entrance of Jezreel" (1 Kgs. 18:46). 1 Samuel 10:5–6 associates possession behavior (the "spirit of Yahweh" comes strongly upon David) with music, and 2 Kings 3:15 suggests that music facilitated Elisha's becoming possessed.

Once again, we can put this phenomenon in a wider context. Reports of shamans employing music to induce states of possession or trance are common. In Siberia the instrument of choice is a drum or tambourine. Shirokogoroff speaks of the drum and rhythmic dancing being used both to produce and to maintain the state of ecstasy (1935, 326, 363–64).[43] Mikhailovskii reports that "the tambourine is met with amongst almost all the Siberian tribes who have shamans; besides its power in calling up spirits, it has the miraculous power of carrying the shaman" (1895, 78). Referring to the Toba people of northeast Argentina, Pablo Wright reports, "Unlike ordinary humans, the shaman can handle visions and dreams at will. He enters into ecstasy through song, rhythm, and, in some cases, dance" (1992, 156, 158). Like Elijah running before Ahab's chariot, performing shamans often display impressive feats of physical strength and stamina. In Siberia they may dance for long periods of time clad in costumes that can weigh in excess of forty pounds, while old and apparently frail Woodlands Indian "conjurers" are reported to have kept their tentlike structures swaying for hours.

Another indication of possession behavior is the encounters of Elijah with a messenger (mal'āk) of Yahweh. Twice during his flight to Horeb such a messenger fed Elijah (1 Kgs. 19:5,7), and in another story the messenger of Yahweh instructed him to confront King Ahaziah's messengers to Baal-zebub and, later, to accompany the captain to see the king (2 Kgs. 1:3, 15). With the exception of the anonymous and treacherous prophet mentioned in 1 Kings 13:18, none of the preexilic prophets reports such a visitation.

It seems clear that the "messenger (mal'āk) of Yahweh" is in many passages best understood actually to be Yahweh, directly perceived in the world by people whom Yahweh wishes to contact. Dorothy Irvin's study, mentioned above, demonstrates this for the narratives of Genesis 16 and 22, and it is also clear from two stories in Judges. In one (6:11–24) a "messenger of Yahweh" greets Gideon, who questions him about the Midianite oppression. At that point Yahweh turns to Gideon and commands him to deliver Israel (vv. 14,16). Gideon prepares a sacrifice, and the *messenger* ignites it and vanishes; Gideon cries, "Help me Yahweh God! For I have seen the messenger of Yahweh face to face." *Yahweh* replies, "Peace . . . you shall not die" (v. 23). The case is similar in the story about an interaction between Samson's parents and a "messenger of Yahweh" who promises them a son (13:2–23). The visitor is also referred to as "a man" (v. 10,11), "a man of God" (vv. 6,8) and a messenger of God (vv. 6,9). In the course of the action, an offering is made to Yahweh, and the messenger of Yahweh ascends in its flames and does not reappear. Manoah says to his wife, "We will surely die, for we have seen *God*" (v. 22). Furthermore, the visitor's appearance was "awe-inspiring" (v. 6). This style of contact with the divine, as well as Elisha's use of music (2 Kgs. 3:15) seems more at home in the conceptual world of shamanism than in Deuteronomistic or priestly Yahwism.

Ecstatic possession or trance may seem out of harmony with what is considered normal prophetic behavior, namely, delivering messages from Yahweh to an audience. One should note, however, that both during and after such experiences shamans may verbally convey information about or messages from the spirits. The shaman may describe the spirits and their travels and activities in other worlds in song or narration. During a shaman's trance, an assistant may put an ear to the master's lips and repeat to the audience what the shaman is saying about the journey of his soul. When he returns, the shaman relates to the audience instructions and information given by the spirits during his soul's journey to the other world.[44] Sometimes when the shaman is possessed, the audience hears the voices of the spirit helpers themselves (Anisimov 1963, in Overholt 1986, 150–58).[45] Sometimes the message concerns diagnosis: "In his state of possession the Tlingit shaman, or his spirit, gave information concerning the remote source of the disease" (Hultkrantz 1992, 59). In Siberia shamanistic performances sometimes conclude with the shaman performing divinations in response to the requests of clan members.[46] We will return to the topic of divination in chapter 3.

Geertz says that "religious symbols formulate a basic congruence between a particular style of life and a specific (if, most often, implicit) metaphysic, and in so doing sustain each with the borrowed authority of the other" (1973, 90). In the process they establish moods and motivations within a conception of "a general order of existence." The actions attributed to characters in the Elijah and Elisha stories mirror this social process. Ahab's accusation that Elijah was a "troubler of Israel" (1 Kgs. 18:17)[47]—along with the widow of Zarephath's angry accusation (1 Kgs. 17:18), Obadiah's wariness (1 Kgs. 18:7–14), the diversion of the king's messengers from the errand on which they had been sent (2 Kgs. 1:2–8), the plea of the army captain (1:13–4), and the appeals of persons in situations of concrete and specific need (for example, 2 Kgs. 3:9–20; 4:1–7, 38–41; 5:1–19)—show people interacting with these men of God as if they were powerful and potentially dangerous persons. The Shunemite's calculating offer of accommodation, her angry demand for assistance, and her attitude of reverence and awe (2 Kgs. 4:8–37) are a particularly good example of the interplay Geertz describes between life-style and a "metaphysic" that embodies the conceptual world of shamanism.

Elijah, Elisha, and the Structure of Israelite Society

With respect to the relationship of belief to action, of social structure to individual agency, one must assume that in monarchic Israel there was no single, normative "faith of the Old Testament" and no clear line of demarcation between official and popular religion. Just as culture is complex, the relationship of a given individual to elements in the culture is complex. The narratives mirror at least two symbol systems—shamanistic and Deuteronomistic Yahwism—and picture Elijah and Elisha as participating in both. Frequently, the shamanic symbols are dominant, and characters in the stories seem willing to call upon whatever religious traditions will further their own interests.

That the cycle of narratives in its present form is in the Yahwistic orbit is indicated by the Deuteronomistic assumptions referred to above. There are frequent references to the deity as "Yahweh," though simply counting occurrences overlooks variables like the length and special contents of episodes (for example, references to the fate of the "prophets of Yahweh" is part of the plot of 1 Kings 18 and accounts for three occurrences). It is important to observe that the heaviest concentrations of the name "Yahweh" are in non-"man of God" passages (1 Kgs. 18:1–19:18, 21:1–29; 2 Kgs. 2:1–18, 3:9–20). Three of the four episodes in which "Yahweh" does not occur are "man of God" or wonder-working episodes (2 Kgs. 4:38–41, 6:1–7, 13:30–21). On six occasions Elijah or Elisha is depicted calling on Yahweh for assistance and receiving it. All but one are associated with an act of power, so these stories may be interpreted in terms of the conceptual world of shamanism.[48]

Yet the stories do not distinguish between official and popular religion as if they were two discrete and largely mutually exclusive entities. The premise of the story about the contest on Mount Carmel is that the people are wavering (1 Kgs. 18:21). The story about the Shunemite woman contains a similar ambiguity. Yahweh is not mentioned at the beginning, in either the woman's calculations or Elisha's interview regarding her reward (2 Kgs. 4:8–17). When she later comes to Elisha at Carmel, she accuses him but does not implicate Yahweh. Still, she swears by Yahweh (v. 30). Late in the narrative, Elisha mentions Yahweh twice, but not directly to the woman. The resuscitation occurs in private, and at its public announcement Yahweh is not mentioned.[49] The Shunemite woman is obviously trying to work one aspect of the cultural tradition to her own benefit by putting Elisha in a position where he is obligated to her. The focus here is on a particular type of action. We need not assume that the building of dedicated guest rooms was normal activity vis-à-vis a man of God, any more than (to revert to an example used earlier) Bathsheba's public bath was normal activity vis-à-vis a king. If our own experience is any guide, however, "currying favor" may well be generic.

The presence of Yahwist ideology is signaled at the beginning of the Naaman episode: The Syrian was a great commander because Yahweh had given him victory (2 Kgs. 5:1; cf. Isaiah 10, 45). Moreover, it is seen in the premise that the cure resulted in the spread of Yahweh's fame among foreigners (vv. 15–19). Still, this ideology does not dominate the action. The suggestion of the captive Israelite servant girl (v. 3) indicates that she was from a segment of the population with ties to Elisha and therefore knew that holy men were healers (v. 8), while the king seems either unaware of this role or unwilling to take it seriously (v. 7).

This meshes with the fact that, although Elisha swears in Yahweh's name (v. 16) and Naaman attributes his cure to Yahweh (v. 15), Elisha offers to perform the cure in order to enhance his own reputation (v. 8b).[50] Elisha refuses Naaman's offer of payment, but the story ends with Gehazi acting secretly and in his own self-interest to collect the fee that is the curer's due (vv. 15–16, 19b–24).

Elijah, Elisha, and the Tensions within Israelite Society

Societies are patterned and persist over time, but they are not homogeneous. Since they incorporate tensions at every level, they must have mechanisms for neutralizing these tensions. Much of what has already been said focuses on the presence of two distinct but overlapping conceptions of reality. What might have been the nature of the tension between them?

Geoffrey Samuel's view that both humans and society operate within a "social manifold" provides one way of looking at this overall situation. Within the flow of a single social context, several different "conceptual frameworks" ("modal states," "semi-permanent currents or vortices . . . existing within the social manifold"; 1990, 13, 59) can be systematically maintained concurrently. These are "internalized selectively by the individual"; they are always changing, and are not identical for all members of the society.

Samuel talks about mechanisms by which societies change. Societies in which shamanism is central tend to be "non-hierarchical," and therefore change cannot be legitimated on an "individual's own authority." In general, change must be based on "communications from the 'other realm,'" mediated through individuals who have contact with that realm via, say, visionary states (1990, 104, 107). The shaman has no power to coerce acceptance. Rather, people will tend to accept the shaman's revelation because it "offers possibilities for use and manipulation for the goal structures already implicit in the social group" (115). Thus, in such societies "the emphasis is on maintaining the appropriate mood and style, as defined by the prevailing set of modal states. If these fail to meet the situation, they are transformed" (117). Political centralization, on the other hand, brings with it a shift in the way authority is conceived. The "spiritual power of the 'other realm,'" formerly accessible to "anyone with shamanic powers, is available only to the ruling lineage" or its agents. "Thus, there is an inbuilt opposition between leader and the shaman, or rather between the modal currents that they respectively represent." The latter approach can be called the clerical, after the "typical religious practitioners" of such societies (126). Clericalized and rationalized religions—Samuel cites Buddhism, Islam, and Christianity, but we could add monarchic Israel—may maintain "the potentiality for a revival of the shamanic process. Recent charismatic and fundamentalist movements within Christianity and Islam are cases in point" (127).

The Elijah and Elisha narratives assume a society in which both these patterns are present. This points to a contradiction at what Stanley Barrett (1984) calls the macro level of society, that is, at the level of the fundamental values and concepts in terms of which social life is organized. In recent years there has been considerable discussion of the transition in Israel from tribal organization to monarchy.[51] Regardless of the details of what took place, it is clear that at this critical juncture the Israelites developed social and political institutions that were new to them. The stories about Elijah and Elisha seem to reflect a continuation of the tensions inherent in such a transition. They depict these men of God as having acknowledged power at the local level and also trying to assert power at the national level. They do the latter not by appealing to institutions or commandments, but by demonstrating contact with the "other realm." It is worth noting that in times of social and political disorganization following initial contact with Europeans, native shamans sometimes became the political as well as the religious leaders of their communities, helping them, as E. Jean Matteson Langdon says of the Colombian Siona, "to maintain their distinct identity and worldview" (1992b, 60).

This interpretation does not require us to see in any of the stories an accurate account of actual historical events. The subtext of these narratives seems to reflect people living in a social situation where both patterns exist, where lines of authority and power are being sorted out, and where people act like people are wont to act, often doing what is expedient and seeking their own advantage. The Shunemite does not need a recommendation to the political powers, but she does need personal help. Elijah seems more opposed to the king than Elisha, but the latter is not always in favor (2 Kgs. 6:24–7:20; cf. 3:13–4), and 2 Kings 8:1–6 has the look of a publicity campaign, championing the cause of the man of God in the royal court.

The situation was even more complicated than so far indicated. The texts suggest that worship of Baal was widespread in Israel (cf. 1 Kgs. 16:31–32, 18:17–40; 2 Kgs. 1:2–8, 10:18–28). Besides its political dimension, this must have had profound implications for the conduct of everyday affairs in an agricultural society. The account of the contest on Mount Carmel, a dramatic ritual showdown in which (from the narrator's point of view) the true God ridicules a phony opponent (18:27) and vanquishes the foe by sending both fire and rain, reflects this complexity. It is not surprising that the tension between religious assumptions about the world reflected in this story comes to a head in a ritual context. Again, we are back to basics with respect to culture and society.

Geertz's essay, "Ritual and Social Change," provides a more contemporary example of the eruption of religious and social tensions in a ritual context. The specific case he discusses is the funeral of a ten-year-old Javanese boy. In the traditional culture of the villages, funerals were an occasion for affirming the syncretism of "Indian, Islamic, and indigenous Southeast Asian elements" in Javanese culture (1973, 147). The boy's funeral, however, was marred by antagonism and confusion. By the time of this particular funeral (1954), Java was becoming more urban. "The simple territorial basis of village social integration and the syncretic basis of its cultural homogeneity" were undermined (148), and national political parties with religious affiliations were further disrupting the traditional syncretism. For Geertz, the disruption of this funeral shows that discontinuities between culture (in his terms, "an ordered system of meaning and of symbols, in terms of which social interaction takes place") and social structure ("the pattern of social interaction itself") are one of the "primary driving forces in change" (144).

From our point of view the interesting thing about this case is that in most respects the social life of the urbanized Javanese peasants was going well. Tensions like those that erupted at the funeral tended to occur in connection with "religious beliefs and practices" (164). The trouble, says Geertz, was that while socially the people of the peasant neighborhoods of the city were "urbanites . . . culturally they [were] still folk." In their new context the meaning of the rite had become ambiguous—its symbols had come to have "both religious and political significance." As a result, the participants "were not sure whether they were engaged in a sacralized consideration of first and last things or in a secular struggle for power" (164–5). The sacral/secular dichotomy is not appropriate to 1 Kings 18; the relevant analogy is that public ritual is a place where fundamental tensions can manifest themselves, and that politics can muddy the waters.

We can note another feature of cultural change. The centralization of government in a monarchy implies an increasing dependence on written records, and Samuel shows the power of literacy to undermine the characteristic shamanic mechanisms for transforming society. Shamanic thought is "analogical," it "operates with approximate schemes, continually adjusted to meet the demands of the present situation." Adjustments take the form of "constant small- and large-scale changes justified through direct access to the realm of the shamanic powers." The possibility of accurate record-keeping that comes with literacy can "destroy this whole way of operating" by exposing inconsistencies in reasoning and encouraging "abstraction within a single rational scheme" (137–38).

The stories about Elijah and Elisha are written, and in their present form are embedded in the Deuteronomic history. We have seen that, taken as a group, they embody competing assumptions about reality. How does one account for the preservation of this body of narratives in the Deuteronomic history, a work that interprets the course of Israel's history from the standpoint of a single, dominant ideology?[52] No doubt some of the narratives were found (or made) to serve the purposes of the Deuteronomists, and perhaps popularity or general familiarity played a role in their inclusion. But suppose we follow Samuel's hint. One of the effects of collecting these stories would surely have been to establish a particular character and pattern of activity for Elijah and Elisha—they were powerful, if somewhat capricious, wonder-workers. Writing the collection down would have had the effect of establishing the consistency of this pattern of actions and offering it for scrutiny and reflection. It is not difficult to imagine that for at least some this scrutiny might undermine belief in these "men of God," whose authority was grounded in the supposed performance of farfetched and even immoral activities like raising the dead, making meager amounts of food great, and slaughtering impudent little boys in a fit of anger (2 Kgs. 2:23–25).[53]

Stanley Barrett speaks of mechanisms that "conceal and neutralize" the contradictions that exist within a society, and it is possible to identify such neutralizing mechanisms in the Elijah and Elisha narratives. Like the shaman, Elijah and Elisha address the need for order and control by appearing to deal with illness and other matters of immediate concern. They may have performed rituals geared to daily life (one possible interpretation of the celebrations at "new moon and sabbath" mentioned in 2 Kgs. 4:23). They seem to have a base of support in the groups known as the "sons of the prophets" (2 Kgs. 2:3,5,7,15; 4:1,38; 5:22; 6:1). In addition, these stories have been enlisted into the service of establishing the legitimacy of the Jehu dynasty. The extent of actual political involvement by Elijah and Elisha is an open question. At any rate, the literary co-opting of these perhaps marginal figures in the service of a religious-political ideology also performs this neutralizing function.

ADDITIONAL ANTHROPOLOGICAL INSIGHTS
INTO THE ELIJAH AND ELISHA STORIES

This interpretation of the Elijah and Elisha narratives has focused on their correspondences with the conceptual world of shamanism. This is not presented as the definitive interpretation of these stories, only one that enriches our understanding of them by suggesting a context in which a number of strange or puzzling features may be understood. Nor does this particular focus exhaust what anthropology has to contribute to our understanding of the narratives. Two recent essays illustrate the latter point.

In hopes of gaining insight into the social context and dynamics that underlie the stories about Elijah and Elisha, Scott Hill examines an ancient and continuing phenomenon in "Palestine and nearby areas," the "'local hero' . . . a man or woman who has been recognized as 'holy' in conjunction with shifting balances in social forces." Almost every village has one or more such persons, who are considered holy by virtue of their supposed "privileged access to power (generally meaning God) beyond the reach of other people." The benefits they provide are both individual and communal. They can influence human fertility, the success of crops and business ventures, and safety in travel and work. Furthermore, "by serving as a projection of a community's identity, local heroes allow that community to express a power that has lain dormant." They receive sacrifices and donations, and have shrines, often associated with hilltops or their tombs (1992, 39–48).

A crucial feature of the social dynamics of this phenomenon is that local heroes "stand, consciously or unconsciously, at a key point of tension between the center and the periphery of power. This positioning is inseparable from the development of their following" (52). Hill discusses a variety of moves at the individual, institutional, and grassroots levels through which the hero's authority is established and maintained. It is important to note that dead as well as living heroes may have authoritative standing in the community. In fact, "resurgence [of authority and power] is in many ways the local hero move par excellence, whether instigated by a central or by a grassroots force. The local hero, being dead, is completely depersonalized, and it is clearly social forces that provide his power." He or she functions as a "wire" through which power flows to "groups or individuals in authority" (63).

Using the local hero model, Hill offers a somewhat speculative reconstruction of Elijah's career. Among other things, he suggests it is unlikely that Elijah was a "straightforward Yahwist," since to attain a position of authority he may have had to strike "the proper balance of local customs, urban Yahwism, and urban Baalism to relate well to various peasant and elite factions." He may have formed an alliance with "a 'wing' of the Yahwists that was more egalitarian and traditionally Yahwist in learning," but it is more likely that the biblical account presents an Elijah who has been "Yahwistized," in effect co-opted (an institutional move) into the service of legitimating Jehu's revolution (66). With respect to the drought theme of the Elijah narratives, Hill observes that control of water sources is "an important part of local hero veneration in Palestine." The narratives are silent on the matter of Elijah's death. In any case, the confrontation on Mount Carmel ensured his vitality as a local hero. "Tied now to a powerful cult, known for a successful act of defiance, and, most importantly, given responsibility for ending an awful drought, Elijah has given the people of Israel something to run with. . . . Thus Elijah was available as a power source in the time of Elisha and Jehu" (67, 71).

Hill moves too easily from comparison to biography. Nevertheless, the social dynamics revealed by his "local hero" model are clearly relevant to the kinds of issues I have raised about these narratives. He does not deal specifically with Elisha, but his discussion of the power of the local hero even after his death, and the importance of the grave as a focal point of the hero's power, seems particularly useful in understanding the otherwise bizarre account in 2 Kings 13:20–21 of the corpse that in a moment of danger was hastily thrown into Elisha's grave, and "as soon as the [dead] man touched the bones of Elisha, he came to life and stood on his feet." The section of Sirach's "praises of famous men" devoted to Elijah and Elisha indicates that such tales can indeed cement the reputation of a dead holy man. Sirach devotes eleven verses to Elijah (48:1–11) and alludes to virtually all the episodes contained in the narratives in Kings. By contrast, only three verses are about Elisha (48:12–14). The first generalizes on the quantity of his miracles ("twice as many" as Elijah), and the last two allude specifically to the brief episode of the resuscitated corpse.

My second example is an essay by Tamis Rentería, a cultural anthropologist, who offers a detailed analysis of the Elijah and Elisha miracle stories using as her theoretical framework a "'culture and power' interpretive analysis" (1992, 79). Employing Raymond Williams's "concept of 'hegemony'" ("a way of thinking and feeling that saturates the everyday lives of particular peoples and that is shaped by a specific experience of power"), she interprets the Elijah and Elisha narratives "as a historical record of the 'lived experience' of a particular people at a specific historical time within the constraints of a particular hegemony, and against the constraints of a particular hegemony" (79. 82).

Drawing on data from Mexico, Rentería sets the miracle stories in the context of peasant religion, which centers in family. Families and villages have patron gods and saints, and rituals center on matters of fertility, weather, survival, and social relationships. Miracle stories told by peasants "appear to celebrate the successful psychological transformation of the social actor who petitions the miracle, moving from despair/skepticism/resignation to triumph over a seemingly insurmountable problem." The characters in the stories are in desperate need, and the stories suggest that significant changes are possible. They are thus "a type of propaganda for the prophet" (1992, 99–100). Stories like those contained in 1 Kings 17:8–24 and 2 Kings 4:8–37 assume (as their "anti-narrative") the "audience's experience" of dealing with exploitative and ineffective prophets. 2 Kings 4:1–7 celebrates the wisdom of following and relying on the prophet, and 4:38–41, 42–44, and 6:1–7 are about the empowerment of individuals (100–12).

Rentería views the stories as tales of resistance. Since they were preserved within a monarchic literature, they are not explicitly against the Omrid dynasty, but they do "reveal glimpses of 'the lived experience of subordination and domination' of people who did not benefit from the monarchic system, and who continued to live according to a cultural reality that implicitly or explicitly challenged the dominant hegemony of an urban-based monarchic Yahwism." She identifies "four different aspects of the dynamics of this struggle between disparate Israelite cultural realities" (113), including the heavy burdens on women, the "transactional relationship" implicit in prophetic activity (the prophet and the community need and have expectations of each other), the "hegemonic struggle" between prophets and kings, and the use of stories about prophets to legitimate Jehu's overthrow of the Omrid dynasty.

Again, this study addresses familiar issues from a somewhat different perspective and contributes significantly to our understanding of the dynamics of miracles and of these biblical stories.

CONCLUSION

In my discussion of the Elijah and Elisha narratives I have tried to avoid the error of focusing on specific elements in the story and interpreting them as normative, historical items of social behavior. Instead, I have focused attention on patterns of behavior, types of activity, that can be discerned in the stories, and have suggested a context that may be of use in interpreting them. As further support for the analogy with shamanism, I offer two concluding comments. The first is theoretical in nature. In his classic study of Siberian shamanism, S. M. Shirokogoroff notes that, despite the existence of a European ideology that takes its death for granted, shamanism lives on as the adaptive complex it always was (1935, 392–93). This observation may be relevant to our understanding of the Elijah and Elisha stories in two senses: In them we catch a glimpse of shamanism adapting to a situation in which Yahwism is becoming dominant; and if this has gone largely unnoticed, it may be in part because of the contemporary reader's ideology that wants to see Yahwism as triumphant, bolstered by the assumption that shamanism is too "primitive" a phenomenon to be found in an urban, agricultural, monarchic society.

The second comment is more practical. In an essay titled, "Elijah and Elisha: Sorcerers or Witch Doctors?," Ernst Wendland points out that among the problems faced by translators of the Bible are difficulties "due to certain crucial differences in worldview, in particular, with respect to the system of basic presuppositions and values that govern human thought and behavior." He goes on to point out that when "considered from the traditional point of view of the Tonga of South Zambia," some elements in the stories about Elijah and Elisha seem to depict them as local curers (mung'anga) and others as "a typical 'sorcerer' or 'witch' (mulozi)." Although not everyone will make such a connection, "there is at least the possibility (and in a few instances the strong likelihood) that a significant portion of the reading or listening public will experience some difficulty in correctly understanding what is going on in the original account" (1992, 214).

Someone viewing Elijah through the eyes of a traditional Tonga would find numerous indications that he was a sorcerer: He utters a curse that results in a whole group being punished (1 Kgs. 17:1). His "mystical familiar spirits" (black, and therefore evil, birds) bring him food (1 Kgs. 17:6; the "meat" would be "the flesh of a recent victim"; 215). No one would dare refuse a reputed sorcerer's request (17:16). "Once a sorcerer has been exposed (through divination), he (or she) will be confronted with the accusation and commanded to reverse his spell" (17:18; since Elijah does not deny the charge, the Tonga would understand him to be admitting it). The sorcerer can undo his magic (17:21; the only difference is that in Tonga practice this would be done in public). Powerful sorcerers are able to hide themselves from attack (18:10), to control "lightning for destructive purposes" (216; 18:38, 2 Kgs. 1:10), and to control whirlwinds for both rapid transportation and for destruction (2:11). "Doctor-diviners" can bring rain (1 Kgs. 18:44–45).

Likewise, Elisha would appear to be a sorcerer. He curses those who dare to offend him, calling his spirit familiars to carry out the curse (2 Kgs. 2:24; in the old translation this impression was heightened by rendering "she-bears" as "hyenas"; 1992, 219). He is a curer (2 Kgs. 2:21, 4:32–37), and in the story about the Shunemite woman's son he acts "like any shrewd *mung'anga*, "first send(ing) his apprentice (alternatively, an animal familiar spirit) to go out on a reconnaissance mission at the site where he will soon perform an act of divination and healing. The purpose is to remove the magical 'mines' of a rival sorcerer" (219). There are many more examples.

Wendland concludes by remarking that while "well-indoctrinated Christians, especially those who are able to divorce themselves from their own social and cultural context when reading or hearing the Scriptures," might not have much difficulty with these passages, "less capable readers" would. "In terms of this more indigenous outlook, the religious beliefs of the ancient Hebrews do not seem to be that much different from their own" (223). Perhaps at one level they were not.

NOTES

1. The wonders that occur in the narratives of Exodus and Numbers are more clearly and consistently attributed to Yahweh, so that the reader does not think of them as miracles performed by Moses or Aaron. Exodus 7:3,5 set the tone: "I will multiply my signs and wonders in the land of Egypt. The Egyptians shall know that I am Yahweh when I stretch out my hand against Egypt." Yahweh is behind both the magic tricks, duplicated by Pharaoh's "magicians" (7:8–9, 17–8; 8:1, 5) and the remaining plagues (8:16, 21; 9:2–5, 13–21; 10:2, 4, 21; 11:1, 4–5). The same is true of the deliverance at the Red Sea (14:13–14, 18, 21, 26, 30) and the episodes about provisioning in the wilderness (Exod. 15:25, 16:4, 17:5–6; Num. 11:31). By contrast, Long points to a group of Elisha miracle stories (2 Kgs. 2:23–24; 4:1–7, 38–41; 6:1–7; 13:20–21) that portray him as "the master magician," in which God is scarcely mentioned (1975, 48). Cf. Rofé's description of what he calls the short *legenda* (1988:13–22).

2. For example, in his interpretation of 2 Kings 4:8–37, Schmitt holds that neither vv. 13–15 nor 29–32, 35 (which he refers to as a "*na'ar* stratum") were part of the original text (1975, 6–8).

3. For example, Fohrer (1957) identified six original Elijah narratives and six later anecdotes in 1 Kings 17–2 Kings 1, and Hentschel (1977) produced an elaborate reconstruction of what he considered to be the genuine Elijah tradition and its elaborations, both pre– and post-Deuteronomistic.

4. For example, Hentschel claims that the combination of the traditions is responsible for the displacement of episodes like the call of Elisha, which now appears in 1 Kings 19:19–21 but was originally part of the Elisha traditions (1977, 53–56).

5. For example, the Ojibwa story called "Clothed-in-the-Garb-of-a-Turkey" (Jones 1919, 195–207) and the Zuni story, "Upo'yona Marries the Daughter of the Village Priest" (Benedict 1935, 2:153–58).

6. Cf. Irvin 1978, 112; Culley 1980; Kirkpatrick 1988, 97–112. In her study of Zuni folktales, Ruth Benedict argues that "the agreement between the conduct of contemporary life and the picture of life in the [Zuni] folktales is very close," though not exact. Nevertheless, she does not believe they can be used as a source for historical reconstructions (1935, 1:xv, xlii–iii).

7. Chapter 4 of Rogerson's book is devoted to a discussion of folklore.

8. Niditch says that "the folklorist's anthropology . . . treats the tale as a dynamic symbolization of worldview and ethos in Geertz's terms (i.e., of the metaphysic, the view of the very structure of the cosmos, and the values, the way of life, tone, style of living). . . . Such literature can serve as an informant if one asks the right questions. Does the material betray certain attitudes to authority? to gender? [etc.] . . . " (1987, 18–20).

9. A whole section of Thompson's *Motif-Index*, E0–E199 (a total of 16 pages), is devoted to "resuscitation" and classifies a large number of variations on this theme. We should note that resuscitation, especially of game animals, is an important element in the world view of hunter-gatherers and in their narratives; see, for example, Overholt and Callicott (1982, 62–75, 139–66). Shamanism is an integral part of this hunting world view.

10. It is possible that references to illness and curing have gone unrecognized in some texts. Citing Akkadian and Hittite parallels, Adrien Janis Bledstein (1992) interprets Tamar's activity of preparing a special kind of food for her brother Amnon (2 Sam. 13:7) as a therapeutic act. The plot seems to depend on her being known to other characters in the story as a person within the royal house "officially designated" to perform a healing ritual.

11. Contrast the Exodus narratives, where wonders demonstrate that there is a *God* in Israel (Exod. 7:5; 8:22; 10:2; 14:4).

12. The episode in which a corpse is resuscitated by coming into contact with Elisha's bones (2 Kgs. 13:20–21) strengthens the idea that touching is a key element in curing; cf. Johnson (1964, 58). Rofé, who considers this story an "ethical *legenda*," contrasts the long-distance cure with the more direct, magical miracle-working of the "simple legenda" (e.g., 2 Kgs. 2:19–22, 23–24; 4:1–7, 38–41, 42–44; 6:1–7). In this story Yahweh "alone has the power to heal" (via contact with Yahweh's "holy land"; 1988, 128).

13. I. M. Lewis, whose objections to overly narrow definitions of shamanism were mentioned in chapter 1 (cf. pp. 16), defines "shaman" as "an inspired prophet and healer, a charismatic religious figure with the power to control the spirits, usually by incarnating them. If spirits speak through him, he is also likely to have the capacity to engage in mystical flight or other 'out of body experiences'" (1986, 88). Accordingly, "shamanism" is "'a cult whose central idea is the belief in the ability of some individuals chosen by some spirits to communicate with them while in a state of ecstasy and perform the functions of an intermediary between the world of spirits and the given human collective'" (92; quoting V. N. Basilov). A recent volume on shamanism among native South Americans echoes some of these themes. Written from the point of view of symbolic anthropology, these essays attempt to go beyond earlier discussions associating the supposed magical rites of shamanism with primitive mentality and shamans with

pathological mental conditions. Shamanism is, rather, "a central expression of the worldview of a culture," a "true institution" that endures and must be studied in both its religious and its social aspects (Langdon 1992a, 10–12).

The vast literature on shamanism can be conveniently sampled by consulting the bibliographies of the works just cited.

14. Similarly, H. I. Smith reports an account of an Ojibwa shaman from the Upper Peninsula of Michigan who pursued the soul of a sick man, brought it back in a "small box," and blew it into the man's mouth, after which the patient became "well again" (1896, 283). In another instance of the same type, a woman's soul had been taken by an angry shaman, Nagaek. "Shawanasowa was more powerful than Nagaek, and in the night went, by superhuman power, several hundred miles to visit him. He obtained her soul, placing it in a small box for safety, and brought it back. He had the squaw open her mouth, and blew in the soul. She recovered and lived to be an old woman" (283–84).

15. Similar accounts of resuscitations can be found in the ethnographic records of other cultures. For example, the !Kung Bushmen (southwest Africa) curer, Old K"xua, told Megan Biesele: "When people feel bad, my friend, I don't dance. But if a person dies,. . . . I carry him on my back and lay him down. I lay him out so that we are lying together. . . . I dance him, dance him, dance him, dance him so that God [Kauha] will give his spirit to me. Then I return from God and put his spirit back into his body" (in Halifax 1979: 60). Among the Cocopa Indians of the lower Colorado River, in stubborn cases of illness due to soul loss the shaman would "lie down beside patient and send own soul to land of dead. Afterwards doctor related adventures" (field notes of E. W. Gifford [1934, 311]). The Huichol Indians of southwestern Mexico believe that one's soul or life force lives in the head. It can wander away during sleep or when one accidentally hits one's head, and once outside the body, it can be captured by a sorcerer or eaten by an animal. Unless a shaman (*mara'akame*) finds it and brings it back, the person will die. When the shaman finds the soul (which is very tiny), she or he wraps it in a bit of cotton and places it in a bamboo tube. The shaman then returns to the patient and puts the cotton on the crown of the patient's head. Then, the shaman Ramon Medina Silva told Peter Furst, "the cotton disappears inside the head with that life. And that man comes back to life again" (in Halifax 1979, 173). Contemporary non-native observers sometimes knew about and reported these beliefs about native shamans. For example, a story in the *Walker Lake Bulletin* (Nov. 12, 1890, during the height of the Ghost Dance excitement) mentions the belief of "several 'good' Indians" that Wovoka, a Paiute shaman and the Ghost Dance prophet, had caused it to rain and had brought a dead girl back to life (Logan 1980, 268–69).

A related phenomenon is the legends about saints who restored the dead to life; these legends can be found in folk traditions associated with the so-called world religions. For example, from Somalia comes a story of a local saint, Sheikh Xuseen of Bale (the framework is "the worldwide Sufi movement," but with "a high degree of local patriotism"), to whom a mother appealed after her small son, an only child, had been devoured by a hyena. The Sheikh "went into spiritual ecstasy, prayed to God and said: 'Oh God, I pray to you that you may take the boy out of the hyena's belly—this is not difficult for you—and that the boy may be alive and walk and go to his bed tonight!' After God had taken him out of the hyena's belly, the woman saw the boy just sleeping by her side in the morning, created the same as he was before, but even more handsome, [alive] and walking" (Andrzejewski 1974, 16, 21). Similarly, songs praise Ramdev, a fifteenth-century Hindu hero-saint from western Rajasthan state, and speak of his miracles, including raising the dead (see *An Indian Pilgrimage: Ramdevra*, a film produced by the South Asian Area Center at the University of Wisconsin-Madison).

16. On this general point, cf. Theodore J. Lewis (1989); Elizabeth M. Bloch-Smith (1992); and Mark S. Smith (1990, 126–32).

17. In light of this interpretation, it is interesting to note that Rofé (1988, 125) considers 2 Kings 4:33b ("and prayed to Yahweh") to be a later editorial addition "from the perspective of the more profound and theologically more advanced strata of biblical thought" displeased with the "primitive religious outlook" that saw miracles "as magical acts that were a manifestation of the prophet's supernatural prowess." In terms of genre, Rofé considers the Elisha narrative to be a "literary elaboration" of the *legenda*, and the Elijah story to be an "ethical *legenda*" (1988, 27–33, 132–35). His interest is in classifying the "prophetical stories" as they appear in the completed Hebrew Bible, not in recovering the details of an anterior ideology.

18. Shirokogoroff notes the strong connection between Manchurian Tungus shamans and the children of their clients. "In a great number of cases . . . the shaman takes the soul of the child (male or female) and keeps it up to a certain age, sometimes up to thirteen or fourteen years. . . . In this function the shaman's spirit is actually a guardian spirit of the child" (1935, 378).

19. There is a (distant?) possibility that this discussion of the shaman's assistant and of the shaman's role as protector of the community can provide a clue to the interpretation of one of the more puzzling episodes of the cycle, the story of how Elisha cursed forty-two "small boys," who were subsequently mauled by two she-bears (2 Kgs. 2:23–4). The term translated "small boys" (*nĕ'ārîm*) is ambiguous. Sometimes it clearly refers to a small male child (e.g., the Shunemite's son; 2 Kgs. 4:29–35), but elsewhere its refers to adult servants, young men who may be field hands (2 Kgs. 4:19, 22, 24) or soldiers (1 Kgs. 20:14–19). On other occasions, as we will see, it refers to the prophets' assistants. If one of the functions of Elisha was to protect his community, and if the offending persons in this story were young men or servants rather than little children, the carnage, though still grisly, would make more sense. Even on this interpretation the story seems greatly exaggerated, but we will see later on that such tales of the "miraculous" have a function.

20. This is suggested by Hosea 2:11 (Hebrew, v. 13), where the topic is precisely the fertility of the land—Yahweh, not Baal gave it, and he will take it away because of the people's misdeeds (vv. 1–13). Other references to a new moon feast (1 Sam. 20:5, 18, 27) or to new moon and sabbath (Amos 8:5, Isa. 1:13) are more general.

21. Other examples of shamans functioning to protect the community

include the following: Among the Siona (Rio Putumayo, Colombia), master shamans used to lead weekly ceremonies "directed . . . to the game spirits, weather spirits, river spirits, or others, depending on the season and needs of the community . . . for the well-being of all," and in addition "special sessions for cases of severe illness, or emergency situations requiring immediate divination of the supernatural forces operating behind the event" (Langdon 1992b, 46). When their hunters are unsuccessful, Eskimo shamans perform ceremonies that seek reconciliation with the game animals and their controllers (Merkur 1985, 4–5). Nyima (a Nuba tribe of the southern Sudan) shamans contribute to the unity of the group at large by providing "a spiritual focus for a community otherwise rigidly divided along lines of descent" (Nadel 1946, in Lessa and Vogt 1965, 472). Baiga (a native tribe in Madhya Pradesh, central India) shamans protect the community from tigers by performing the Mati Uthana ceremony after someone is killed by a tiger (Elwin in Overholt 1986, 253–57). Culina shamans (Amazon River, western Brazil) "lead rituals at birth and death that protect the community from the dangers posed by these events" (Pollock 1992, 27; at birth a baby lacks a soul and is open to various dangerous influences, 36; at death the shaman has to conduct the deceased's soul to the underworld so that it poses no threat to the village, 36). They also provide for success in hunting.

22. "Mack Winnemucca said that the Paviotso killed sorcerers . . . who caused people's death" (Lowie 1924, 294). Gifford (1934, 310) documents this practice among the Cocopa.

23. For earlier suggestions of a connection between Elijah and Elisha and shamanism, cf. Kapelrud (1967), Goldammer (1972), and Long (1975).

24. Cf. the discussion of LaFargue, pp.20–21 above. "Mind-set" does not refer to a conscious or willful intention on the part of an author, but rather to factors that control the author's mind and give "a particular character to the differential system which is (the author's) life-world." Such factors "function . . . in the same manner as grammatical 'competence' functions, that is, by allowing a native speaker of English to differentiate between 'The girl saw the bird' and 'The bird saw the girl.'" As the author's mind was shaped, so the reader's mind ought to be shaped by this "competence." This means that "the difficulty for interpretation is not the indeterminacy and ambiguity of texts, but rather the fact that their meaning is so determinate and particular that no paraphrase can substitute for engagement with the words themselves and their particular background" (1988, 353–54). My argument is that a socially and historically situated experience of prophetic/shamanic activity forms part of the life-world and mind-set of the authors of these narratives. Needless to say, one can understand this code or mind-set without sharing the beliefs it implies.

25. According to Hultkrantz, "shamanism is deeply anchored in the old hunting cultures with their individualism, animal-spirit beliefs and hunting symbolism." In agrarian cultures it declines in importance, but it "has nowhere completely disappeared" (1978, 51, 53).

26. For an extended discussion of this aspect of the Elijah and Elisha narratives and parallels in Paiute and Siberian shamanism, see Overholt 1989, 86–111; cf. Long 1975.

27. L. Bronner offers a different interpretation, seeing all such stories about Elijah and Elisha as counterattacks against Baal. They were not "invented by popular story-tellers," but were assembled by a "theologian," a "well-informed author," as polemics against Canaanite mythology (1968, 139–40). Her argument is particularly weak with respect to the resuscitation stories: In the Ugaritic texts Baal dies and is resurrected, and knowing this, the people of Ugarit "perhaps believed that Baal . . . had the power to resuscitate others," though this is never said explicitly in the texts, and no humans are even to be found in the Baal cycle (116). She notes that Anat promises eternal life to a human being, Aqht (who, by the way, scoffs at the idea). Anat has Aqht killed to get the coveted bow, then seems to mourn his death. The text is broken at this point and does not say that Aqht is revived, but Bronner assumes he is. On the basis of this evidence Bronner says, "The writer of the stories of Elijah and Elisha was well acquainted with the belief that prevailed in Ugarit that Baal who died and was resurrected could resuscitate. With his stories he demonstrates that the God of Israel controls life and death" (119).

28. Concerning Siberian shamanism, Shirokogoroff says that "tricks" are to be understood as demonstrations of "personal power" and not "as imposture and tricking of the audience." The goal of both tricks and divination is "to convince the audience"; they create a convincing context for self-suggestion and hypnotism (1935, 331, 332).

29. The only exception is Isaiah 38:7–8. I am excluding from this discussion the wonders attributed to Moses at the time of the exodus and in the wilderness.

30. See C. Schaeffer (1969). Like Hallowell, Schaeffer supplements more contemporary observations with older reports by European-American witnesses of the ceremony. One of these is from Peter Fidler, a Hudson Bay Company surveyor, who in 1793 witnessed a performance during which the shaman learned the whereabouts of a band member who was absent and overdue, and correctly stated the reason for the delay and the time of his eventual return (1969, 4–5). John Cooper tells of an old Gros Ventre woman whose "ghost helper" revealed the whereabouts of stolen horses and the men who went in pursuit of them, as well as details of their condition and arrival back in the camp. The next day's events proved her information correct (in Overholt 1986, 74–76).

31. See the discussion above. Goldammer (1972, 271–74) speaks of shamanistic elements in the narratives about Moses and mentions Moses' staff. The narratives about the escape from Egypt mention a wonder-working staff (usually wielded by Moses, but sometimes by Aaron or Pharaoh's "magicians") twenty-four times (Exodus 4–10, 14, 17; Numbers 20), though the term used, *maṭṭēh*, is different from that used to refer to Elisha's staff (*mišʿenet*). The latter term is less frequent, and the eight occurrences outside 2 Kings 4 clearly indicate that it refers to a walking stick. The former term is much more frequent (252 occurrences in the Hebrew Bible) and has a wider range of meanings: tool, royal insignia, an instrument for exercising power, "staff of bread" (always in a negative sense—a broken "staff of bread" equates with "famine"), and even "tribe." As we have seen, acts of power are a stan-

dard part of the repertoire of many shamans, and the staff of the Exodus narratives appears to have affinities with this phenomenon. The royal-political connotations of *maṭṭēh*, however, suggest another avenue of interpretation. The figure of Moses as it is presented in the Hebrew Bible seems to me less susceptible to interpretation in terms of the world view of shamanism than do Elijah and Elisha.

32. This translation is conjectural; the Hebrew reads, "the young man the young man the prophet."

33. Episodes using only the title "man of God": 1 Kgs. 17:17–24; 2 Kgs. 1:2–17; 4:1–7, 8–37, 38–41, 42–44; 6:1–7; 6:24–7:20; 8:1–6, 7–15; 13:14–19. Episodes using only the title "prophet": 1 Kgs. 18:1–46; 19:1–18; 2 Kgs. 3:9–20; 9:1–13. Episodes using both titles: 2 Kgs. 5:1–27; 6:8–23. Episodes using neither title: 1 Kgs. 17:2–7, 8–16; 19:19–21; 21:1–29; 2 Kgs. 2:1–18, 19–22, 23–25; 13:20–21.

34. It is worth noting that the account of the contest on Mount Carmel contains the only mention in the cycle of the people's violation of the "commandments of Yahweh" (*miṣwōt-yhwh*), a standard prophetic/Deuteronomic theme (1 Kgs. 18:18).

35. The phrase occurs only once outside the cycle, in 1 Kings 20:35. Cf. Wilson 1980, 140–41.

36. R. Wilson also understands Elijah and Elisha to have been peripheral prophets (1980, 194–206).

37. 2 Kings 4:1, 38–41; 5:19–24; 6:1–7; cf. also 4:42–44. The widow with whom Elijah stayed was poor, though not Israelite (1 Kgs. 17:12). The general designation of supporters in 1 Kgs. 19:19 (seven thousand faithful Yahwists who have not worshipped Baal) clearly establishes the group as peripheral but reveals nothing about social status.

38. Cf. Wilson 1980, 5–8; see also his discussion of the distinction between two "mechanisms of intermediation," possession by a spirit and trances involving soul loss or migration (32–42).

39. Wilson (1979) argues for the association of possession behavior with the writing prophets; Parker (1978) argues against it.

40. For example, Exod. 9:3, 13:3; Deut. 2:15; 1 Sam. 5:6, 9; 2 Sam. 24:14.

41. Similarly, Ezek. 3:22–24, 8:1–4, 37:1, 40:1.

42. See Ezek. 1:3, 3:22, as well as Isa. 8:11 and Jer. 15:17.

43. Cf. also Anisimov 1963, in Overholt 1986, 150–58; Lopatin 1946–49.

44. Cf. Mikhailovskii 1895; 66–67, 77; Shirokogoroff 1935, 328.

45. In the Ojibwa shaking tent ceremony, the spirits speak loudly and distinctly enough to be understood by the audience outside the structure, and Hallowell comments that this "provides tangible validation of basic concepts about the nature of the dynamic entities of the cosmos, familiar in belief and myth" (1942, 85; Hallowell does not believe these ceremonies entailed the possession of the shaman by the spirits—cf. pp. 12–13). Kracke (1992, 131–32) describes a Kagwahiv (western Brazil) ceremony similar to the shaking tent involving two shamans. One is out of sight in a structure and receives spirits, the result, it is thought, of his traveling to the sky. The other is outside interpreting

for the audience, in stereotypical terms, the behavior of the spirits. Shirokogoroff also mentions that spirits speaking through the shaman are an important source of the people's knowledge of the spirits (1935: 162).

46. Anisimov 1963, in Overholt 1986, 157; Mikhailovskii 1895, 95, 99, 126, 140–42, 149; Shirokogoroff 1935, 315.

47. This is not the only passage in which the verb "trouble" (*'kr*) carries ominous religious overtones. In Josh 6:18 and 7:25 breaking a taboo is the cause of Israel's trouble; in Judg. 11:35 and 1 Sam. 14:29 (cf. v. 24) an oath is the cause.

48. 1 Kgs. 17:21–22, 18:36–8; 2 Kgs. 2:24, 4:33, 6:17–20; the exception is 1 Kgs. 19:4–8.

49. This is in contrast to the parallel story in 1 Kings 17 where the widow, though a foreigner, mentions Yahweh by name (v. 12). The cure is private, but her public acknowledgment affirms Elijah as a true spokesman of Yahweh (v. 24). Yahwist ideology is much more in evidence here than in 2 Kings 4.

50. This is in marked contrast to the wonders associated with the exodus from Egypt, where it is Yahweh's reputation that is at stake (cf. note 1, above), but in harmony with the activities of shamans seeking to enhance and maintain their position within the communities.

51. The literature is extensive. See, for example, Gottwald, ed. (1986), Coote and Whitelam (1987), and Flanagan (1988).

52. There has been much discussion of the problems posed by the Elijah-Elisha cycle of narratives as we find it in the books of Kings. A. Rofé tends to focus on developments over time in the forms employed in the individual units. Thus the "short *legenda*"—episodes like 2 Kgs. 4:1–7, 38–41, and 42–44 that present miracles "as magical acts" and express "a primitive religious outlook"— are sometimes altered in an attempt to make them more theologically pleasing, and new forms like the "ethical *legenda*"—for example, 2 Kgs. 5 and 1 Kgs. 17:8–16 and 17–24, where miracles are intended not as a benefit to individuals but "to increase and spread the belief in God, even among other nations"—are created under the influence of later prophets (1988, 125–35). Long views the individual episodes in terms of their literary context in the books of Kings, which he assumes to be "a substantially unified, singly authored work deriving from the exilic period of Israel's history, after 587 B.C." (1984, xv; on specific episodes cf. 177, 182–83, 187, 202–03; 1991, 22, 51, 61–62). To give one final example, Todd argues that the Elijah and Elisha "cycle of stories was constructed in a way that gave legitimacy 'without any doubt' to Jehu's reign in Israel." The legends were "pulled together" and written down after Jehu's rebellion "to authenticate Elisha's prophetic role in the revolution as well as the revolution itself" (1992, 1–2).

53. Long makes a similar point with respect to the "contrary tendencies" in the story of the Shunemite woman (2 Kgs. 4:8–37), which can be read as either "Elisha-centered or Shunemite-centered," depending on the particular features of the text to which one responds. "Perhaps one is meant to temper that unreflective awe before the prophet whose power and authority have seemed unquestioned to this point. . . . Homage is due this prophet, but also reserve, for his power has seemed in need of moral restraint and his knowl-

edge has seemed deficient" (1991, 61–62). Wesley Bergen puts the matter even more strongly, arguing that this story presents us with a prophet who does miracles that are unrequested and unnecessary and who must be constrained by a socially powerful woman to act responsibly (n. d.). Elsewhere, Bergen argues that the Deuteronomic history is careful to show his relationship to the king in such a way as to eliminate Elisha as a proponent of a system that would rival the monarchy (1992a). So also Mary Shields, who says, "the story as a whole presents a subtle critique of the man of God and his wonder–working" (1993, 66).

III

Anthropological Views of Israelite Social Roles and Institutions

DIVINATION IN ISRAELITE SOCIETY

Many people, ancient and modern, have found in divination a useful means "of communication with the supernatural forces that are supposed to shape the history of the individual as well as the group" (Oppenheim 1964, 207). A wide variety of techniques for making inquiries of the supernaturals have been invented and employed, from examining the entrails of sacrificial animals (for example, in ancient Mesopotamia), to interpreting cracks in bones that have been held in a fire (China, native northeastern North America), to casting lots. The common denominator is that one relies on the knowledge of a specialist to gain information not ordinarily available to humans about things or events—past, present, or future.

The Hebrew Bible makes it clear that the ancient Israelites used divination. To cite but a few of the many examples, we read that lots were employed to apportion the land among the tribes (Josh. 18:6–10 and often), to assign roles to the goats in the Day of Atonement ritual (Lev. 16:8–10), and to settle disputes (Prov. 18:18). Oracles were consulted before going to battle (Judg. 20:18–28; 1 Sam. 23:4, 28:5–7), to identify a guilty party (Josh. 7:10–26; 1 Sam. 14:38–42, where the Urim and Thummim are specifically mentioned), and to seek assurance about physical complaints (Gen. 25:22; 1 Kgs. 14:1–3; 2 Kgs. 1:2–4, 8:8). Samuel cast lots to determine the identity of Israel's first king, Saul (1 Sam. 10:20–24). Joseph possessed a cup that he used in divination (Gen. 44:5). Numerous texts simply assume the presence of diviners as one of the component groups within Israelite society (for example, Isa. 3:1–4, Jer. 29:8, Micah 3:5–8, 1 Sam. 28:3–7, 2 Kgs. 17:17). Proverbs 16:33 states the assumption that must have lain behind such activities:

> The lot is cast into the lap,
> but the decision is Yahweh's alone.

Although divination seems to have been important in Israelite society, our understanding of its function is hampered both by the lack of detailed descriptions of divinatory acts in the Hebrew Bible and by the negative attitude toward it reflected in certain prominent texts. Deuteronomy 18:9–14 is the prime example of this point of view. Eight types of divination are listed by name, but no information is provided about the techniques characteristic of each or the occasions on which Israelites might have consulted a diviner. Rather, divination is simply condemned, along with child sacrifice, as belonging to those "abominable practices" of the nations that the Israelites must not imitate. These foreign peoples, the text says, recognize "soothsayers and diviners," but Yahweh does not allow Israel to do so.[1]

This text might be taken to imply that all divination was banned in Israel. Certainly the passage that follows immediately (Deut. 18:15–22) makes the "prophet like Moses" the chief, if not the only, agent of communication between Yahweh and the people. But such a picture cannot represent any actual state of affairs. In the first place, the text itself is not quite a blanket statement prohibiting divination, since it does not mention the use of dreams, Urim and Thummim, and lots, all well known in the Hebrew Bible. In addition, texts outside Deuteronomy indicate that all of the forms of divination it does prohibit were actually used at one time or another in Israel's history. Finally, though these foreigners, Israel's neighbors in the land of Palestine, did practice divination—some texts in the Hebrew Bible recognize this and accept it rather matter-of-factly[2]—F. Cryer concludes on the basis of an etymological investigation that the specific terms for divination in Deuteronomy 18:9–14 are "virtually without exception either first derivable from Hebrew itself or from Mesopotamia; but not . . . from Israel's 'neighbors'" (1994, 261).[3]

A look at the immediate context of the condemnation makes it clear that it is part of the Deuteronomists' picture of an ideal Israel whose social and political existence is governed by a more or less pure form of Yahwism, uncorrupted by the practices of the people the Israelites displaced. Deuteronomy 17:8–13, for example, gives instructions for resolving judicial cases in which the decision is "too difficult for you." In such a situation one should go to Jerusalem and consult (*drš*) "the levitical priests and the judge who is in office in those days," who will announce a decision. The activities proper to these officials are "instructing in the law" (*tôrāh*) and "speaking a decision" (*mišpāṭ*, v. 11), and the punishment for failing to carry out their decision is death (v. 12). It seems significant that the verb *drš*, is often used of consulting a god by means of a diviner (18:11—"inquiring of the dead") or prophet (1 Kgs. 22:5–8, 2 Kgs. 22:13). The contrast with Deuteronomy 18:9–14 is clear. It is priests and judges, and not diviners, who are the officials to whom one must come for the resolution of difficult matters.

Deuteronomy condemns divination as a foreign practice, and the sections immediately before and after that condemnation contain the same theme. The prophets "like Moses," who will serve as intermediaries between Yahweh and the people and whom people must obey, are thoroughly Israelite. They will be raised up from among their own people, and they must speak in the name of no other god than Yahweh (18:15–22). Similarly, the rule regarding the king (17:14–20) combines permission to choose a monarch from among the people with an explicit prohibition against selecting a foreigner. In this larger context, then, the Deuteronomists are setting forth their ideal view of the proper personnel for the regulation of society in Yahweh's Israel and the proper methods for settling disputes and contacting the deity. Diviners are not an "official" part of their scheme. Diviners were, however, present, and we will need to search for clues in order to assess divination's actual place in Israelite society.

The View from Within

The Hebrew Bible assumes that various forms of divination were practiced in Israelite society, but (apart from condemnations) does not specifically discuss its social location or describe the details of its practice or its rationale. The many and scattered references to the phenomena of divination do, however, allow us to construct the following tentative picture.

It appears that a main function of divination was to provide knowledge relevant to the well-being of king and nation. There are several references to the use of divination at the time of accession to the throne: Saul was selected by lot to be Israel's first king (1 Sam. 10:20–24), and on the basis of an oracle David journeyed to Hebron, where he was anointed king of Judah (2 Sam. 2:1). Divination could also be an important part of preparing for and conducting military operations. Saul (1 Sam. 14:37, 28:6), David (1 Sam. 23:2, 4; 2 Sam. 5:19, 23), and Ahab and Jehoshaphat (1 Kgs. 22:5–6) all "inquired" of Yahweh before entering battle. Tribal groups during the premonarchic period employed the same kind of divination (Judg. 1:1; 20:18, 23, 27).

David consulted a priestly oracle during the period of his conflict with Saul (1 Sam. 22:10, 13, 15). There are reports of inquiries made of Yahweh in the midst of a military campaign when decisions had to be made or difficulties were encountered (1 Sam. 30:8, 2 Kgs. 3:11), and after the campaign one could use divination to divide the booty (Joel 4:3, Obad. 1:11, Nahum 3:10). Inquiries were made at the king's request concerning the future prospects of the nation (2 Kgs. 22:13, Jer. 21:2).

The role of divination in establishing and maintaining Israelite social order is evident in the accounts of the allotment of the land and the Day of Atonement ritual. In addition, disputes could be settled (Prov. 18:18), guilt determined (Josh. 7:16–26), the possibility of success of an undertaking assessed (Judg. 18:5), and the appropriate time for actions determined (Esther 3:7, 9:24) by means of divination.

Divination also functioned at a more personal level, where it was employed to determine the causes of family welfare (Gen. 30:27) or threats to personal well-being (Jonah 1:7) and to help recover lost property (1 Sam. 9:5–10). Persons sometimes inquired of an oracle concerning illness or other physical complaints (Gen. 25:22; 2 Kgs. 1:2, 8:8).

Several of the passages cited with reference to the social functions of divination speak of someone inquiring of Yahweh by means of a prophet, and this raises the question of the social location of divination in Israel. There is clear evidence that at least some Israelite divination occurred in a cultic context. Leviticus 16:8–10 shows that the casting of lots was part of the Day of Atonement ritual, and Joshua's casting lots "before Yahweh" (Josh. 18:6–10, 19:51) suggests that this procedure was a part of the established cultic apparatus. One also notes Micah's mention of sorcerers and soothsayers in a list that includes images, pillars, and Asherim (5:9–14 [English 10–15]); cf. 2:5). Similarly, Micah's generalized attack on corrupt religious officials associates diviners with other cultic peronnel like seers, prophets, and priests (3:5–11).

Divination could be performed by a specialist in a particular technique (for example, 1 Sam. 28:7–14), but it was also performed by priests and prophets. Micah draws a particularly close connection between prophecy and divination when in a single utterance he uses the same term (*qsm*) to refer to diviners as a separate category of cultic personnel (3:7) and to the message and activity of the prophets as "divinations" (3:6; NRSV translates "revelation") and "divining" (3:11). Priestly divination could occur at a regular sanctuary (1 Sam. 22:9–19, Nob) or wherever the need arose and the requisite equipment was available (1 Sam. 14:16–19, 36–42; 30:7–8). Connection with a sanctuary seems not to have been a factor when divination was performed by a prophet (1 Samuel 28:6, 1 Kgs. 22:5–28,; 2 Kgs. 3:13–19:, 8:7–10,

22:13–20; Jer. 21:2–7). Nor does the "mistress of a ghost" who conjured the ghost of Samuel at Saul's request (1 Sam. 28) appear to have done so at an official cultic site.

With respect to the social location of divination we should also note Isaiah 3:1–3, which includes diviners in a long list of roles important to the stability of society, including soldier, judge, prophet, elder, dignitary, and counselor. Similarly, the context of Micah 3 associates prophets and diviners with "rulers" (v. 11). It seems likely that popular forms of divination existed outside the cult and official circles, though we have little information about them (cf. Gen. 25:22, Jonah 1:7).

Divination, then, appears to have been a firmly established part of Israelite society. Still, we have noted that certain segments of the population, no doubt overrepresented in the present Hebrew Bible, harbored a deep hostility toward it. Some texts consider the practice of divination a capital offense (Lev. 20:27, 1 Sam. 28:3–9). Others list it in conjunction with a variety of cultic infractions (Lev. 19:26, 2 Kgs. 23:24, Isa. 19:3) or other kinds of lawbreaking (Mal. 3:5).

The Hebrew Bible provides us with some indication of the various techniques of divination and the dynamics of consulting a diviner. We frequently hear of a casting or drawing of lots, though an exact description of this procedure, especially of the equipment used, is impossible. The description in Leviticus 16 of selecting the goats for the Day of Atonement ritual, the numerous references in Numbers 26–36 and in Joshua 14–21 to apportioning the land, and the scattered references to dividing booty all use the term *gôrāl*, "lot." Divination with the Urim and Thummim (1 Sam. 14:36–42) may be a type of judgment by lot involving drawing two stones, one light and the other dark, out of the hem of a garment.[4] Drawing lots may also be behind the process of selection described in Joshua 7:16–21 and 1 Samuel 10:20–21, which speak of a group being "brought near" and one member of that group being "taken." Divination could also make use of dreams (1 Sam. 28:6, Dan. 2:2), the ark (Judg. 20:27), or an ephod (1 Sam. 14:17–19, reading with LXX; 23:9–12; 30:8). The reference to Joseph's cup (Gen. 44:5) suggests divination by reading patterns formed by drops of oil floating on water.

As to the dynamics of the consultations, the usual practice was for someone to approach a diviner with an inquiry to be placed before Yahweh. Thus Saul consulted Ahijah (1 Sam. 14:18) and, under pressure during his last campaign against the Philistines, a variety of oracles (1 Sam. 28:6–8). David consulted Ahimelech at Nob (1 Sam. 22:10) and later Abiathar (1 Sam. 30:7). Typically, the questions have binary form: Should I go to battle against the enemy or not? (Judg. 20:23, 27; 2 Sam. 5:19, 23; 1 Kgs. 22:6, 15); Shall I pursue the enemy/go up to such and such a place or not? (1 Sam. 30:8, 2 Sam. 2:1); Did the man come here?

(1 Sam. 10:22); Will the enemy attack? (1 Sam. 23:11); Will I recover from this illness? (2 Kgs. 8:8). The basic problem posed in questions like, Who shall go first? (Judg. 1:1, 20:18), To which city shall I go? (2 Sam. 2:1), and To which group does the one being sought belong? (Josh. 7:16–21; 1 Sam. 14:41–42, 10:20–21) could be solved by asking an extended series of questions in binary form. Ezekiel's description of Nebuchadnezzar's advance toward Jerusalem (21: 23–28 [English 18–23]) is another example of this process of selecting between alternatives.

Sometimes one encounters a series of divinations pursuing an answer in a step-by-step fashion (Josh. 7:16–18; 1 Sam. 10:20–21, 23:9–12; 2 Sam. 2:1), and subsequent divinations may be made to test the results of a prior one (1 Sam. 23:1–3, 1 Kgs. 22:5–18). Apparently more informal ways also existed by which people could evaluate the results of divination, such as judging whether the results tended to further the diviners' self-interest (Micah 3:5–7) or whether the information produced by a diviner tended to be accurate (1 Sam. 9:6).[5] Finally, several texts mention diviners' fees (Num. 22:7, Micah 3:11).

Evidently, the indigenous interpretation, of such procedures—the Israelite view—was that divination provides the inquirer with new and reliable knowledge, the source of which was God. As well as in Proverbs 16:33, the same sentiment is implied in two texts that use the analogy of divination to assert the trustworthiness of other persons. One comments on the esteem in which a royal counselor was held: "Now in those days the counsel that Ahithophel gave was as if one consulted the oracle of God" (2 Sam. 16:23, NRSV; literally, "consulted the word of God"). The other is a proverb extolling the king's justice:

> Inspired decisions [literally: divination] are on
> > the lips of a king;
> his mouth does not sin in judgment.
> > (Prov. 16:10)

In this same vein, Isaiah can describe Yahweh's intention to turn the desolate land of Edom (following the destruction Yahweh will bring upon it) into a permanent residence for all manner of wild animals as an act of divination: "he has a lot (*gôrāl*) for them" (34:17).

Proverbs 16:33 also reveals why many forms of divination involve the manipulation or inspection of some physical phenomenon. In theory, at least, such things as which lot is taken in a blind draw; the patterns of birds in flight, drops of oil on water's surface, and cracks in scorched bones; configurations of the entrails in sacrificial animals; and so on ad infinitum are free from human manipulation and therefore can be taken to represent knowledge from the realm of the divine.

1 Samuel 28:3–7 seems to make a qualitative distinction between

types of divination, suggesting that some (dreams, Urim and Thummim, and prophets) are within the bounds of Yahwism, while others (mediums and wizards) were prohibited. According to this narrative, however, even though Saul expelled the latter two groups from the land, he had enough confidence in their veracity to consult a medium when the more standard forms of divination proved inconclusive.

We have already noted that prophets could be consulted for purposes of divination. Prophetic utterances can be referred to as "divinations" (Micah 3:11; Jer. 14:14; Ezek. 13:6–9, 22:28), and both prophets and diviners can be said to "prophesy" (Jer. 29:8–9; cf. 27:8–10, where the reference is to prophets and diviners from surrounding kingdoms). Such texts suggest that ambiguity concerning the exact boundary between prophecy and divination was another element in the indigenous interpretation of the latter phenomenon.

As we would expect, some texts declare that Yahweh is able to frustrate the work of diviners and undermine the truth of their divinations (1 Kgs. 22:19–23, Isa. 3:1–3). Still, in ancient Israel it appears that one could have confidence in diviners and in the results of their procedures.

A Broader View

To this point we have established the presence of divination in Israelite society and suggested something about its functions, character, and meaning. But we have also noticed that divination is an uneasy presence in the Hebrew Bible, where it is sometimes vehemently opposed. This conflict of opinion, together with the paucity of detailed information about divination, presents some problems for our understanding of Israelite religion. One of these has to do with the relationship between prophecy and divination. How does one explain the apparent similarity between what prophets and diviners do? Another problem, critical though less often raised, can be expressed in the question, What kind of world view is required to make belief in divination credible?

What assistance can we hope for from comparative ethnology in our efforts to understand Israelite divination and suggest solutions to problems like these? At a general level, comparisons can help us see how "normal" Israelite divination was. It is not something bizarre, but a practice we would expect to find in one form or another in a preindustrial society like biblical Israel. Here I refer the reader to an earlier study in which I show that elements of Israelite divination as it is portrayed in the Hebrew Bible are in basic harmony with the phenomenon of divination known to us in a variety of modern, preindustrial cultures. These elements include the remuneration of diviners for their services, the belief that gods established divination as a way to communicate with humans, the kinds of motivations that lie behind a resort to divination and the expectations about what knowledge may be obtained through it, and the critical evaluation of diviners by their clients (Overholt 1989, 131–36).

Comparative ethnology can also suggest solutions to specific problems, such as the relationship between prophecy and divination. It is not surprising that the Hebrew Bible, which in its present form is so heavily influenced by a Deuteronomistic-prophetic point of view, displays a bias in favor of prophets, conceived of as intermediaries whom Yahweh sends and through whom Yahweh speaks directly, and against diviners, who when consulted employ some expert technique to determine the deity's will. The implication is close at hand that while diviners have the potential to manipulate the outcomes of their procedures to their own benefit, the directness of Yahweh's word to the prophets is a protection against such fraud. Modern interpreters have often shared this bias, sometimes postulating an evolutionary scheme in which early divination was eventually replaced by prophecy (cf. Cryer 1994, 241–43).

We have already seen that this basic distinction is over-tidy. Israelites did consult diviners in hopes of obtaining knowledge, but they also consulted prophets for the same purpose (for example, 1 Sam. 28:6, 1 Kgs. 22:5–28, 2 Kgs. 22:13–20, Jer. 21:2–7). Divination was usually performed at the request of a person who came seeking information, but could also be initiated by a diviner (1 Sam. 14:36–37). Several narrative texts suggest that it was Yahweh who initiated a divinatory procedure (Josh. 7:14, 1 Sam. 10:17–21). In 1 Samuel 10:17–27 the same proceeding includes both a divination-like oracle (Yahweh speaks through the sacred lots) and a prophet-like one (Yahweh speaks directly; it is not said through whom). In 1 Samuel 9:1–10:16 the diviner, Samuel, is not simply a technician, but a person through whom Yahweh speaks and who is free to enlarge the scope of the consultation beyond what the client, Saul, originally intended (learning the location of some lost livestock) to matters affecting the kingdom. Other narratives contribute to a sense of the ambiguity of the line dividing prophet from diviner by expanding the results of divination beyond the standard "yes," "no," or "inconclusive" to include utterances that seem prophet-like (cf. 2 Sam. 5:23–24, 1 Kgs. 22:19–23, 2 Kgs. 22:16–20, Jer. 21:3–7, Ezek. 20:3–44).

These observations suggest two questions that we can put to ethnographic accounts of divination. The first is: How much control do diviners have over the outcome of their divinations? One of the prominent features of divination as it is practiced in many cultures is that it tends to be rule-bound. This has the effect of limiting, if not altogether eliminating, the diviner's ability to influence the outcome of the consultation. Sometimes the procedures are quite elaborate. In Ifa divination, practiced by the Yoruba and other West African peoples, the diviner throws eight palm nuts, notes the resulting pattern, and then recites a series of verses that are traditionally associated with that pattern. Not only would it be physically difficult to manipulate the fall of the nuts, but the rules of the procedure are well known by both clients and other diviners, who would criticize any deviation from them. As an additional safeguard, clients often do not tell the diviner the reason for their consultation and themselves select the applicable verse from those the diviner recites. The verses that stand as the core of Ifa divination form a body of tradition of such importance that William Bascom has referred to them as the "unwritten scriptures" of the Yoruba (1969, 11, 121). Bascom (1967) observes that in two variants of Ifa divination that have made their way from Nigeria to Cuba, written instructions now exist in notebooks. Here we have a kind of textual regulation of divination analogous to ancient Mesopotamian omen lists, which existed in written form and introduced a degree of regularity into the interpretation of omens.[6]

Other, simpler forms of divination lack such elaborate controls. Among both the Navajo Indians of the American Southwest and the Kuba of Zaire, a diviner may simultaneously recite a list of words appropriate to the particular consultation (causes of disease, for example, when the task is diagnosis) and perform a physical activity, arm trembling and rubbing a disk on an oiled surface, respectively. The word being uttered at the moment the arm stops trembling or the disk sticks is considered the answer to the client's query. On the surface it would seem much easier to manipulate procedures like these, but diviners routinely deny that they do so and their clients for the most part believe in the validity of the oracles.

In practice, the process of a divination consultation often involves an extended give-and-take between the diviner and the client, and the "meaning which emerges" is negotiated through that interchange (Peek 1991a, 70). Ifa consultations, for example, can be quite lengthy and involve a large number of questions to which the diviner responds by casting the nuts and reciting verses associated with the various patterns. Diviners may attempt to influence the interpretation by improvising a verse or reciting a verse ordinarily connected with another pattern. It is the client, however, who chooses from those verses the one he or she considers applicable to the situation at hand (Bascom 1969, 50–71). Among the Batammaliba of Togo, a lengthy interchange takes place between the diviner and an "adviser" who represents the client. The adviser asks questions, sets out possibilities for the diviner to accept or reject, and checks the veracity of the diviner's answers against his own knowledge of the circumstances that motivated the consultation. But the diviner is also free to suggest alternative avenues of questioning that the adviser should pursue (Blier 1991, 79–89).

To cite one more example of such dialogue, when the Yaka of northern Zaire consult a mediumistic diviner, great care is taken to preserve the client's anonymity. The affected person is not present, but is represented by an "intermediary object" and one or more human representatives, who respond tersely to the diviner's statements so as not to reveal any information. In a trance the diviner carries on a dialogue with the representatives in which the diviner must first determine the cause of the visit and then suggest links between the problem situation and elements of the traditional Yaka world view having to do with the etiology of life-giving and life-harming forces. Thus, "the message of the oracle presents itself [to the clients] not only as something credible, but also as something self-evident and unassailable, when the diviner reveals facts that are unquestionably part of the particular problem situation." In the end, "the oracle brings about the meaning of the unknown by laying bare the hidden coordinates of the problem situation in reference to the relevant higher-order axiological system, and allows in this way for efficacious intervention" (Devisch 1991, 117, 130).[7] All of this suggests that the results of divination tend not to be controlled in any simple way by the subjectivity of the diviner.[8]

In forms of divination that rely on random occurrences—for example, scapulimancy, in which cracks and scorch marks are produced by holding the shoulder blade of an animal over a fire—or on spirit possession, there would seem to be less possibility of standard results, and thus more opportunity for the results to be heavily influenced by the diviner's (and the client's) knowledge of the circumstances surrounding the consultation. Still, a variety of practices serve to safeguard the results of divination from outright manipulation. For one, the apparently random configurations of cracks on a heated bone are frequently interpreted by reference to stereotypical patterns and conceptions (cf. Speck 1977, 142–43, 155–63; Vollweiler and Sanchez 1983, 199–201), and the same is true of the South African practice of casting divining "bones" (Dornan 1923). The Zulu test the genuineness of a diviner's possession by hiding things that the diviner must find (Callaway 1991:,33), and the Yaka have a similar test in which people ask the diviner to identify what they are holding in their closed fists (Devisch 1991, 115–16). Furthermore, the account of Yaka divination given in the preceding paragraph indicates that mediumistic divination may operate within boundaries and is not simply a matter of subjective manipulation.

In general, ethnographic accounts suggest that diviners typically view themselves, and are viewed by their clients, as providing valid knowledge from an extrahuman source. Like all knowledge, however, it can only be grasped by means of an act of interpretive appropriation by a human mind. In this respect the situation is little different from prophecy. Despite the claim made and believed that the words a prophet speaks come directly from a deity, the subjective interpretation of both speaker and hearers must always be assumed. This accounts in large part for the difficulty biblical scholars have had in defining firm criteria for distinguishing "true" from "false" prophecy.

Another question we can put to ethnographic accounts of divination is whether there is typically a well–defined distinction between a prophet-like role (in which a person claims to receive messages from a deity and transmit them to an audience) and the diviner's role (in which the deity's will is discovered with the aid of some special technique). Evidence indicates that often there is not. Three observations are germane on this point. First, much has been made of prophets' special calling to their role, but diviners frequently claim (and their audiences expect and acknowledge) similar experiences in which deities recruit them into their role. Zulu and other diviners are selected by being possessed by a spirit (Callaway 1991; Rigby 1975, 121), and the Lobi of Burkina Faso (formerly Upper Volta) believe persons are coerced by spirits into accepting the role of diviner (Meyer 1991, 93–94; most people resist this call, since the work load is heavy and the tangible rewards meager). The future diviner of the Ixil Maya (Guatemala) has a series of call-dreams that both reveal to individuals that they are to be diviners and give them specific knowledge they will need in their practice (Colby and Colby 1981, 58–72; cf. Shaw 1991, 143). Often, external symptoms allow both individuals and the public at large to recognize a person's designation by some supernatural power to take up the role of diviner. Among those symptoms recognized by the Yaka are a particular kind of wasting sickness, heightened fluency with the language, sharpened imagination, loss of self-control, and the ability to perform physical feats such as jumping to the roof of a hut in one bound (Devisch 1991, 114–17).[9]

Second, like prophets, a number of diviners lay claim to direct communications from a deity, often manifested in trances during which a spirit possesses the diviner and speaks directly through him or her (cf. Rigby and Lule 1971, 22–37; Turner 1975, 209–75 *passim*). It is not unusual to find societies in which diviners of this type coexist with those who employ more mechanical methods.[10] It is interesting to note that the Yaka consider the mediumistic diviners to be more reliable (less open to the manipulation of results) than the more mechanical rubbing-board and poison oracles, and therefore consult them in more serious cases (Devisch 1991, 113).

Third, we have reports from cultures as widely separated as Siberia, Japan, tribal India, and Native North America of inspired intermediaries like shamans being called upon to perform divination. A good example of this overlapping of functions comes from Uganda. Traditional Kiganda society included both diviners and prophets, the former concerning themselves largely with the affairs of individuals and the latter with affairs of state. It was possible, especially during times of crisis, for a single individual to perform both of these roles. Peter Rigby (1975) provides an example of one such person, who was already functioning as a diviner when he was possessed by one of the important national gods and instructed to move his base of operation to that deity's national shrine. There he continued to divine, but also in those years just prior to Ugandan independence he performed national prophetic functions such as advocating the expulsion of the whites and the return of the king and of the old religion.[11]

The conclusion to which the anthropological data lead, and which I have argued in more detail elsewhere, is that prophecy and divination are variant forms of the same phenomenon, religious intermediation— that is, a process of communication between the human and the divine spheres in which messages in both directions are channeled through individuals who are recognized by others in the society as qualified to perform this function. The dynamics of this social process can be described in terms of a pattern of interrelationships between a deity, a religious functionary, and an audience that in its essential characteristics is the same for both prophecy and divination (Overholt 1989, 17–25, 140–47). We might explain the fact that in some societies both forms exist by suggesting that in the process of communication, prophecy is the "natural" mode for deities to initiate contact with their people, and divination is the "natural mode" for people to contact the deities. Since both are part of the mainstream religious enterprise, the personnel can overlap.

In societies where they exist, both prophets and diviners are believed to be intermediaries between deities and humans. People persisted in this belief despite the fact that the oracles they received must often have proven inaccurate or unhelpful. No doubt they continued to consult these intermediaries because they believed the process worked, and such a belief would be grounded in a particular way of understanding the nature of reality.

Another contribution of comparative ethnology can be to shed some light on the kind of world view required to make belief in divination plausible for people who hold it. In the introduction to a collection of essays on African divination systems, Philip Peek writes:

> Divination sessions are not instances of arbitrary, idiosyncratic behavior by diviners. A divination system is often the primary institutional means to articulating the epistemology of a people. . . . The situating of a divination session in time and space, the cultural artifacts utilized (objects, words, behaviors), the process of social interaction, and the uses made of oracular knowledge all demonstrate the foundations of a people's world view and social harmony. Divination systems do not simply reflect other aspects of a culture; they are the means (as well as the premise) of knowing which underpin and validate all else. (1991a, 2)

Although it is impossible to find a single world view shared by all societies in which divination is practiced, some generalizations seem permissible. For one thing, such societies share an underlying assumption that supernatural forces shape events in the world and that these forces are able and willing to communicate their intentions to humans. As Oppenheim puts it, people in ancient Mesopotamia believed that these gods were "interested in the well-being of the individual or the group" (1964, 207), and the gods are sometimes explicitly credited with setting up the systems of divination through which this communication takes place (for example, the god Ifa established the system that bears his name; McClelland 1982, 41).

This assumption can manifest itself in a variety of ways, depending on the social organization of the particular society. During the late Assyrian Empire, the assumption had political ramifications—"the real ruler of the state was the god," the king was the god's earthly representative, and divination was a means of "revealing the approval or disapproval of the god" (Pecirkova 1985, 156). At the other extreme are the Lobi, hoe-farmers and small-scale cattle breeders of Burkina Faso, whose principal source of social authority is a class of voiceless spirits (*thila*) who communicate through diviners. The *thila* are believed to be directly involved in looking out for the welfare of the community, even to the extent of "forcing certain individuals to open markets in specified places or to organize collective hunts" (Meyer 1991, 93).

A second generalization is that the view of causation assumed in such societies is different from that to which we are accustomed. To give a specific example, Devisch tells us that the Yaka employ both "linear" and "structuralist" notions of causality. The former attaches importance to accidents, contaminations, and other tangible antecedents to certain effects. The latter ignores the temporal dimension and relates the effect to "a relatively uniform etiological grid" that factors in data about the client's matrilineage, beliefs about curses and the cults that support them, and the like (1991, 112–13, 123–24). In this way

> The oracle connects the submitted illness with some recent infringement or abuse, or some quarrel involving the sick person . . . and also an analogous situation in the history of the uterine descent. This connecting of present and historical situations is not causalist but metaphoric and brings to light an important dimension of the meaning of the problem. It is as if reference were made to the self-maintenance of social life and to a unifying, all-embracing, and axiological horizon of meaning and order. (Devisch 1991, 128)

A recent study by Frederick Cryer addresses this issue of causality by placing divination within the more inclusive category of magic. In particular he rejects any attempt to view magic as protoscience and to distinguish between those acts that are rationally or empirically based and those that are based on faith, since cultures that practice magic do not themselves make such a distinction. The "interpretation of magical behaviour," he says, "has to be based on features *internal* to the society in question, such as native symbolic actions and utterances, statements of native belief and exegesis of their own behaviour, and so on." One can "conjecture that magical practice is always logically intelligible when seen 'from within'" (1994, 92–93).

Cryer argues that magical actions like divination are best understood as "performative 'utterances'." They are "conventional social acts" comprised of two parts: a "socially pre-established situation" in which the action takes place, and certain words or other behavior appropriate to that situation.[12] The question one asks a diviner in effect becomes a "verbal model" of reality, and the diviner's answer "may be interpreted as a promise . . . which the gods themselves have pronounced." Thus, divination is an "act which affirms or denies a symbolic representation of (projected) reality." In societies that practice divination, "there is no question but that it works, which is to say, that the members of the society regard it as giving valid information." At the same time, we must understand that a society that regards divination in this way has not "arrived at a stringent understanding of cause and effect which in any way corresponds to the understanding(s) of causation adhered to in 'empirically' oriented societies." In terms of this underlying epistemological issue, the difference between this world view and our own is absolute (1994, 117–22, 188, 208, 332).

Anthropology, then, succeeds both in making divination more familiar (we can recognize it as normal in a culture like that of biblical Israel) and in reinforcing its strangeness (in terms of epistemological differences from our own). In both respects it can help clarify our interpretations of the Hebrew Bible texts.

WOMEN, SMITHS, AND KINGS

The argument of this book has been that research by anthropologists who have studied relatively modern cultures can often be useful to persons interested in understanding the culture of ancient Israel. In this final section I will discuss briefly the work of several scholars who have made productive use of anthropology to study issues other than those dealt with above. The aim is not so much to summarize the contents of these books as to provide further illustrations of how such material can enrich our interpretation of texts and suggest solutions to problems that textual evidence alone is insufficient to resolve.

The Status of Women in Premonarchic Israel

We begin with Carol L. Meyers, whose *Discovering Eve: Ancient Israelite Women in Context* (1988) was motivated by a feminist concern to learn more about women in the biblical tradition. Meyers's chief interest is in the lives of "'ordinary' Israelite women." But where does one get the information needed to construct a picture of "Everywoman Eve"?

The most obvious source of information, the Hebrew Bible itself, proves to be disappointing, since it displays an androcentric bias and reflects the urban context and elite institutions of its authors. Only a few women figure substantially in it, and they are for the most part exceptional, not ordinary, persons. The way of life of Everywoman is not directly reported.

Since, Myers's subtitle suggests, her goal is to see "Eve" in the context of "the experience of Israel in the ancient Near Eastern world" (4), another potential source of information is archaeology. In fact Palestinian archaeology has turned in recent decades from a preoccupation with monumental structures to an examination of village life. As a result, we now have a much clearer picture of "patterns of domestic architecture that dominated Israelite settlements" and of the "agrarian economic foundations" of ancient Israelite life. But again there is a problem, since artifacts in and of themselves are not "gender noisy." One needs "ancillary pictorial or textual evidence" in order to distinguish "the domestic tasks performed by men and women in ancient villages" (18–19).

Methodologically, this is where social scientific research becomes important. At a general level, anthropology helps overcome our own modern, urban, industrial bias by showing us the characteristic features of premodern societies like that of ancient Israel. On the specific issue of gender roles, comparative ethnography helps interpret clues found in biblical texts and Palestinian artifacts, suggesting "some probabilities as to which roles always fall to men and which to women in similar societies" (19). In principle, "sociology and anthropology have identified sets of social phenomena that can be linked to particular social settings. Insofar as those settings can be shown to be analogous to the conditions of Israel's existence, some of the gaps in our knowledge can be filled inferentially" (10).

Meyers sets the stage for her reconstruction of "Everywoman Eve" by addressing two issues, one conceptual and the other environmental. The first is the widely shared perception that the Bible is the product of a patriarchal society and "portrays women as secondary or inferior to men in fundamental ways" (24). Her critique of this notion of patriarchy is two-pronged. In the first place, this view tends to equate patriarchy with male dominance and to apply "contemporary feminist standards" to "the cultural patterns of an ancient society" (26). To do so, however, overlooks the point established by anthropological studies that there is no pattern of universal male dominance. It also ignores the fact that "the dynamics of gender hierarchy . . . are historically specific." Gender differences are socially constructed, and are therefore likely to have a "functional role in any specific cultural setting" (29, 36).

In the second place, the standard conception of patriarchy fails to distinguish between the culturally sanctioned authority of men "to make decisions and command obedience" and the power, frequently exercised by women, "to effect control despite or independent of official authority." This is an important distinction because it undermines "the notion that sexually stratified arrangements leave women helpless" (41). For although in many peasant societies the subordination of women is "legally sanctioned," they are nevertheless able to "exercise power and influence significant decision-making." Although one cannot speak of gender equality in such societies, they are characterized by "functional gender balance," or "functional nonhierarchy (44–45)."[13]

The description of the environmental setting relies heavily on data from Palestinian archaeology. Premonarchic Israel was a series of communities made up of individuals who had survived the disasters of disease and warfare of the late Bronze Age and had come as pioneers to the mountainous and heavily forested central hill country of Palestine. In order to make this new ecosystem with its rather poor soils and rugged topography suitable for dry land farming, trees had to be cleared, and cisterns and terraces constructed. The difficulty of this task was exacerbated by the isolation and economic independence of many of the Israelite villages, which required the production of grain in an area more suited to viticulture and olive orchards. All of these tasks were labor intensive. At the same time, since there was no permanent military class, men would often have been called on for military service.

What were the implications of such a setting for gender roles in premonarchic Israel? Anthropological studies indicate that group survival depends on "three basic kinds of activities: reproduction, defense, and the production of subsistence goods" (56). The first of these is the responsibility of females and the second, for the most part, of males. The balance of responsibilities with respect to the last can shift, but the labor-intensive agriculture of the hill country villages (the need to clear land, build and maintain terraces, cut cisterns, and the like) would have drained off male energies from daily production activities. This would have had a double impact on women: they would have been more involved in production and at the same time been called on to bear more children to augment the work force (61). The crucial complementarity of gender roles would have enhanced the social status of women.

Meyers's detailed exegesis of Genesis 2–3 reveals "paradigms for female roles" that fit nicely with this environmental context, though they contrast markedly with standard interpretations of the narrative. These chapters belong to the genre "creation myths," and thus "present the *essential* (archetypal) features of human life" (80). Among these features are the inextricable relationship between "human existence . . . [and] that which makes life possible, arable land" and a "nonhierarchical relationship between" the human genders (82, 85). Genesis 3, dominated by a concern for food, has the form of a "wisdom tale." The poetic fragment embedded in this tale (3:14–19) mirrors "the material basis for human life in the highlands of Palestine," with the phrase "by the sweat of your brow" (3:19) capturing "for all time the intense labor required to grow cereals in that environment" (93). In this context the point of 3:16 is not the subordination of women to men, but rather the essential role of women as producers of food and children. Thus, the narrative of Genesis 2–3 "provides an etiological response to the precariousness of Israelite life" in the period before the monarchy (84).

In her discussion of the family household, the "immediate and determinative social context" for the life of Everywoman Eve (122), Meyers reviews textual and archaeological evidence with respect to the size, configuration, and economic needs of residential groups and anthropological data on the importance and function of households in tribal societies. Excavations of highland villages suggest that each household unit engaged in virtually the "complete range of activities essential for subsistence." In such a situation "the range of tasks was maximal and could not have been accomplished without the active involvement of all household members" (144–45). Comparative ethnography suggests that while some tasks tend to be gender-specific—food preparation, for example, is usually associated with women and plow agriculture with men—others, "including horticulture and animal husbandry," are less so (148). The important point is that in "a peasant or folk society" such as premonarchic Israel, one finds less "hierarchical differentiation . . . [than] in more complex societies" (168–69). While there are advantages to a "division of labor along gender lines," such "gender differentiation, particularly in a society living at subsistence level, implies complementarity and hence interdependence" (172). Questions of female power and male authority must therefore be addressed from the perspective of their functional role in society.[14]

The advent of monarchy in Israel "meant the gradual end of a society in which the household was the dominant social unit," as well as "a gradual demographic shift from country to city" (190–91). Such developments tended to undermine the former relative parity in gender relationships, and Meyers comments briefly on this change.

By themselves the biblical texts fail to provide sufficient information on which to base conclusions about gender roles in premonarchic Israel. Some are so ambiguous as to invite interpretations congruent with post-biblical, even distinctly modern, values and views about gender relationships. Faced with this problem, Meyers set out to fill in "some of the gaps in our knowledge . . . inferentially" (10). The result is a reconstruction of Everywoman Eve which offers a plausible interpretation of Hebrew Bible texts that would scarcely have been possible without insights derived from the data of archaeology and anthropology.[15]

Iron in Israelite Life and Thought

Paula McNutt's *The Forging of Israel: Iron Technology, Symbolism, and Tradition in Ancient Society* (1990) provides a good example of how one might use anthropological theory and field data to throw light on a particular problem, in this case the role of the new technology of ironworking in the development of biblical Israel. The very nature of the problem means that two sources of data are available from the ancient world: references to iron in the Hebrew Bible and in texts from surrounding cultures, and iron artifacts discovered in the course of archaeological excavations. Even so, the combined evidence from these sources is insufficient to answer the question she poses, and she turns to anthropology for help in analyzing the information that results from literary and historical investigations.

McNutt frames the issue by asking, "What kind of impact did the introduction of iron technology have on ancient Israelite culture, and how is this impact reflected in the use of iron technology as a cultural symbol?" (19) The first half of this question suggests issues of material culture. Once the process of carburization was discovered and its use became routine, iron was used to produce truly superior tools and weapons. This development must have had important social, economic, and political consequences for the new nation Israel, though probably not those that have often been thought. Archaeological evidence now suggests that, contrary to the implication of 1 Samuel 13:19–23, the Philistines had no monopoly on ironworking in Palestine. Further-more, while there is evidence of intentional carburization dating from the twelfth and eleventh centuries B.C.E., artifactual data indicate a one-to-two century lag between "the discovery of ironworking" and its implementation in economic activities (158). This means that the set-tlement of the Palestinian highlands and the development of terrace agriculture there, as well as the period of political domination by the Philistines, occurred before any substantial increase in the number and distribution of carburized iron implements.

In the final analysis, it is unclear what role iron technology played in the "consolidation of a united Israel under the leadership of Saul, David, and Solomon" (209). Nevertheless, "whatever the mechanism by which iron technology was ultimately adopted in ancient Syro-Pales-tine, the coincidence of its acceptance with the rise of the Israelite state was a significant factor in Israel's later portrayal of its development as a people under the guidance of the national God Yahweh" (211).

For McNutt, the real issue is not material culture alone, but the interrelationship between material culture and the way in which ancient Israelites thought about their world (35). What she wants to do "is to shed light on how the adoption of this technological innovation later affected Israel's understanding of itself as a people and how this was expressed symbolically in the sacred stories and texts preserved in the Hebrew Bible" (21).

The methodology she uses in pursuit of this goal is "a multidiscipli-nary/integrative approach drawing on the disciplines of biblical inter-pretation, archaeology, and anthropology" (20). Israelite archaeological and textual materials "are treated as 'informants' of ancient Israelite society that can supply us with 'ethnographic' data." Insights from anthropology, in the form of "comparative ethnographic material from contemporary African societies and . . . theories on symbols," are used "as heuristic devices for illuminating the relationship between the archaeological and literary categories of information and for proposing hypotheses about systems of meaning" (36). Thus the book contains a long chapter on African ethnography, followed by chapters that give a detailed account of the development of iron technology in the ancient Near East generally and more specifically in Palestine during the early Iron Age. These form the basis for an analysis of "biblical symbols," in which anthropological theory—Sherry Ortner's "key symbols" and Victor Turner's understanding of the "ritual process"—plays a significant role.

In order to understand her interpretation of biblical symbols, it is necessary to refer briefly to McNutt's account of ironworking in contemporary traditional cultures in Africa. From her study of the ethnographic literature, she suggests some general conclusions about how and why "iron technology [was] appropriated and translated into symbols that are essential elements in cultural systems of meaning" (82). Basic to these is the observation that the transformation that takes place in the process of smelting, carburization, and forging iron is analogous to that in the ritual process of a rite of passage. People who live in "communities in which iron technology plays a significant technological and economic role" will be likely to make the analogy, consciously or unconsciously, between ironworking and rites of passage, so that "symbols associated with ironworking" will function as "key symbols" that illuminate "many aspects of human social experience." The effective symbol is thus grounded in an analogy between important, but different, social processes (82–87).

In these cultures, the smith is viewed as a mediator who effects the mysterious "transformation of iron." As a result, he may be given "other quite varied roles in which he also functions as a mediator," for example, as the officiant who performs circumcisions in rites of initiation. This function places smiths in a "boundary position" that in part accounts for their marginal position in many societies. "The primary function of symbols associated with ironworking in Africa, then, is that of mediation." This is the process that the symbols evoke and clarify (87–95).

The situation appears to be similar in the ancient Near East. There, Bronze Age texts refer to iron objects as precious items of trade, and recognize the material's heavenly origin (meteoric iron). The texts show that meteors and similar phenomena "were regarded as messages from the gods, and as such served as symbols of mediation, although their symbolic quality derived from quite a different understanding than that indicated in Chapter 2 for smelted iron among African societies" (138). Furthermore, one can note that like "typical . . . smiths and artisans in contemporary West African mythology, Enki (Ea) and Kothar are deities whose primary mythological roles are associated not only with providing tools and weapons and introducing and organizing civilization, but also with mediating conflicts (or potential conflicts), advising other deities, and mediating such oppositions as those between heaven and earth, divine and human, and major and minor deities" (234).

In the Hebrew Bible, iron most often "symbolizes power, strength, and durability, all properties derived from the transformation that occurs in the ironworking process. The fact that the end product in the process is so much stronger than the soft ore with which the process begins contributes to the efficacy of these symbolic representations" (219). But there are other associations. God is sometimes referred to as the divine smith, who purifies and transforms Israel (for example, Isa. 1:25, 48:10; Ezek. 22:17–22). Cain, "the culture hero in Israelite myth," is similar to such figures in West African mythology in being considered "the eponymous ancestor of smiths (i.e., the Kenites)" and in his position as a "marginal and ambivalent figure in Israelite mythology"—a murderer and agriculturalist, who is "ancestor of both city-dwellers (Enoch) and tent-dwellers (Jabal)" (240). Similarly, the marginality of the metalworking Rechabites, revealed in Jeremiah 35:6–10, is "reminiscent of the typical position of metalsmiths in African societies," and the story of Jael the Kenite in Judges 4 reflects a "kind of marginal political status [that] is also common among ironsmiths in East Africa, who often provide weapons for both parties engaged in warfare" (243–44).

McNutt takes up the theory of William F. Albright and others that the Kenites were "a group of nomadic or semi-nomadic metalsmiths" (242) and assumes that the Midianites, to whom they were related (Moses' father-in-law, Jethro, is called both), performed a similar social function. This allows her to speculate on alternative interpretations of two difficult stories, Yahweh's attack on Moses (Exod. 4:24–26) and Phineas' murder of the Israelite man and his Midianite wife (Numbers 25). With respect to the first, the role of African ironsmiths in ritual circumcision suggests that Zipporah took the responsibility "for carrying out the circumcision because she is a Midianite from a smithing clan." At this point in the narrative, Moses is on the verge of returning from the desert to Egypt, "another symbolic realm." Thus, the placement of the story may also have "structural significance," for "this is an appropriate place in the overall structure of the exodus narratives to include a rite of passage" (246). In the second story, the apparent seriousness of the sin with the Midianite woman (the sexual liaisons of Israelite men with foreign women were being punished with a plague, which stopped after the death of the Midianite woman and her husband) could be accounted for in light of African notions that "intermarriage with individuals from smithing clans is dangerous and polluting." Moses, married to a Midianite, is "exempt from the condemnation imposed on other Israelites in the biblical traditions" because he "himself is a mediator, and his role as mediator is related to his association with the Midianites" (246–47). These are examples of how the appeal to anthropological analogy may prove useful for solving small puzzles of interpretation.

McNutt's study of biblical symbolism culminates in an examination of the metaphor of Egypt as an "iron furnace." It is commonly recognized that this metaphor refers to the oppression suffered by Israelites in Egyptian bondage, but what we now know about the process and symbolism of metalworking suggests that "oppression is but one facet of the *transformative* quality of the Egypt/exodus traditions. It is this process of transforming that is conveyed most powerfully in the metaphor" (250). Egypt as "iron furnace" is "an 'elaborating symbol' or 'root metaphor'" that "communicates in condensed and tacit form information about the development of Israel as a religious people" (250; she notes the similarity to forge imagery among the Fang of West Africa, "which symbolizes on one level the relationship between past and present"). The meaning of the metaphor is implicit, condensing "information that is treated as self-evident truth by those for whom it has meaning, in this case a 'truth' associated with the transformative power of the ironworking process" (250, after Mary Douglas).

In this interpretation "the processual structure of rites of passage . . . serves as an appropriate analogy for revealing the implied structural relationships (whether made consciously or unconsciously) underlying the iron furnace metaphor and its referents" (251). Indeed, the structure of the metaphor of Egypt as "iron furnace" mirrors that of a rite of passage—a previous state ends with a symbolic death that results in a transitional or transformative period, followed by rebirth into a transformed state. This is precisely the same structure (see McNutt's chart on p. 252) characteristic of ironworking (soft metal/forging/strong metal), the broad historical periods of ancient Palestine (late Bronze Age/early Iron Age/Iron Age from 922–586), and the "narrative perspective of 'history'" in the Hebrew Bible (the ancestral period in Genesis/Israelites in Egypt and the wilderness in Exodus-Deuteronomy/Israel in the promised land in Joshua-Kings).

In addition, "encapsulated in the literary roles of the Midianites and Moses" is the symbol of "metalsmith as mediator," the meaning of which "is not fully apparent unless viewed in relation to the iron furnace metaphor" (255–56). In the narratives of the Pentateuch "it is the Midianites and Moses as Midianite who mediate the transitions in the narrative and the processual structure underlying it." Midianite traders set up Joseph's role as marginal mediator, and Midianites (Jethro, Zipporah, and Moses himself, who married into Midianite society) have a role in the traditions about the exodus and wilderness wanderings. This "structural role of the Midianites is clarified" by analogy with "the smith's role" as mediators and socially marginal arbiters in African societies (256–60).

This, then, is the result of illuminating "ancient information . . . by the ethnographic information from contemporary societies" (261):

> The metaphor of Egypt as an iron furnace . . . serves in the Deuteron-omistic traditions as a root metaphor for ordering Israel's religious development, as an implicit source of categories for conceptualizing and expressing the interrelationships of the events that led to the birth of a nation out of the iron furnace of Egypt. Encapsulated in the metaphor is an awareness of the structural congruence among the domains of iron technology, history, and narrative tradition and the transformations that are represented in each. Implied in the metaphor is the mystery of the Divine Smith's transforming power and the mystery and transforming power of the covenant relationship that forged Israel into a people united as well as the parallel transfor-mation undergone during the Babylonian exile. Condensed in this powerful symbol is the *meaning* of Israel's relationship to God in the past, present, and future. (260)

The Rise of the Monarchy in Israel

This book began with the observation that some stories in the Hebrew Bible—for example, the resuscitation of the Shunemite woman's son (2 Kgs. 4)—are difficult to understand. I argued that an anthropological approach could in many cases assist one in interpreting them. On the other hand, narratives like those in the books of Samuel that tell of the reign of Saul and David's rise to power seem on the sur-face to be straightforward historical accounts. Yet even here an appeal to anthropological data and theory can enhance our understanding.

In recent years a number of scholars have written about the rise of the monarchy in ancient Israel from a self-consciously social scientific per-spective. Among those who make systematic use of anthropology in their research, both James Flanagan and Frank Frick have argued that the centralization of authority in Israelite and Judean societies as the monar-chy emerged can best be understood as the rise of a chieftaincy. Their lines of argumentation leading to this conclusion are somewhat differ-ent, but both make significant use of comparative materials and provide a good illustration of how this strategy can enhance our understanding of an important transitional period in the history of ancient Israel.[16]

As the subtitle of his volume indicates, a modern technological process, holography, provides Flanagan with "a metaphor for the processes and relationships that constitute a social world" and, ulti-mately, with "a model for a social world research design" (1988: 79, 80). His discussion is long and intricate, and he devotes considerable

space throughout his book to explicit reflections on method. Nevertheless, the lines of his argument and the nature of his contribution
can be sketched in brief.

It is obvious that our two main sources of information about Israel in
the early Iron Age are archaeology and the biblical narratives. The data
we encounter through the first of these derive from the "domain of
actions" and the second from the "domain of notions." Since "neither
the Bible nor Iron Age archaeology offers the interpretative framework
for understanding the other" (75), the problem is to understand the
relationship between these two kinds of information.

Flanagan advocates a "truly interdisciplinary" study of the Israelite
Iron Age using "a two-stage model." First, techniques standard to the
disciplines of textual and archaeological studies are used to establish separate images. These "masters" are then integrated, illuminated, and
interpreted with the aid of a holographic model (86–87). Materials from
"comparative sociology"[17] come into play "at the second-level interdisciplinary stage where the comparisons illuminate the images of the past
generated separately by the other disciplines" (116). Comparative materials are, so to speak, the "illuminating beam" of the hologram (82).

Flanagan's examination of archaeological evidence begins with a discussion of the topography, ecological zones, and weather of "ancient
Cisjordan." Next, he analyzes occupation patterns, and finds that "no
universal pattern of L[ate] B[ronze]/Iron I discontinuity and continuity
pervades the area, and no single date for the transitions from LB can be
set" (149). Instead, between Middle Bronze I (ca. 2000 B.C.E.) and Iron
IC (the period of David) several dramatic shifts occurred in population
with "contemporaries in each phase interacting constantly and symbiot-
ically," so that "Iron IC culture . . . incorporates forms and traditions
from all of its predecessors rather than building upon a single culture or
society identified with Iron IA population" (162, 168).

To interpret this evidence, Flanagan turns to comparative materials
from several periods and locations. First, he employs L. Marfoe's analysis of diverse land use and social patterns in Iron Age Lebanon as a
"preliminary archaeological systemic model" for interpreting the data
from Iron Age Cisjordan. According to this model,

> agricultural risks are reduced by mixing cultivation and husbandry and
> by forming social networks that extend across production zones at vari-
> ous elevations on the plains and in the mountains . . . that could save agri-
> culturalists and pastoralists in times of drought or political devastation.
> The unpredictable and uncontrollable nature of affairs produce dynam-
> ic rather than static traditional societies whose basic socioeconomic
> instability and demographic fluidity are related to the ecology. (168)

In such a situation, security is more important than profit, economic and residential patterns compete and evolve or devolve at each other's expense, and classifications of relationships are constantly being juggled. He then turns to modern ethnographies of Bedouin and North African groups for living examples of how these strategies work to spread risks and establish relationships among segments of a society. The resulting model of society in Iron IC Palestine "explains tensions and transformations by making them part of the symbiotic relationships existing among disparate groups living as segmented tribes in extremely varied environments" (187).

Flanagan begins his analysis of textual evidence with the Amarna letters, which reveal the chaotic state of Canaanite society, "a fundamentally maladaptive system" (194). When he turns his attention to the literary images of David in biblical texts, he looks not for history, but for "storyworlds." The goal is to distinguish "the invariables in the David tradition from the variables, i.e., the qualities and actions that all the users attributed to David as contrasted with things writers felt free to change, omit, or add" (196–97). The result is a series of models of the David figure as it appears in the Psalms, Chronicles, the Deuteronomistic history, and the books of Samuel. These "models are ancient holograms," each containing an image of the whole David figure. Although different in emphasis, they each "illumine the same fundamental transitions" (249–50). In these versions of the figure of David he "stands as a mediator always remembered for being in the betwixt and between. . . . The perspective of this hologram is Yahwist, and David is portrayed as the founder of the religion's tradition in Jerusalem" (271–72).

Having relied largely, though not exclusively, on standard disciplinary methods in his lengthy analysis of data from the domains of actions and notions, Flanagan draws heavily on anthropology in a concluding section in which he seeks "a coherent multidimensional image—and for the processes that shape it—by integrating the separate analytical and systemic images from archaeology and literature and by illuminating their intersections with relationships from better known and observable societies" (276). The result is "a hologram of the early Iron Age," a reconstruction of "the social world of David's drama" (273, 275).

Information from anthropology on the nature and polity of segmented societies proves to be the key to understanding the sociopolitical situation in which a David could rise to power in a time and place where monarchical city-states were in decline. As these monarchies devolved, "segmentation [was] crucial for peace and social stability" (280). What all segments of society would share was "a desire for equilibrium and stability . . . [and] leadership that is successful in achieving it for one segment would be recognized and envied by the other[s]" (285). Chieftaincy is a kind of "limited centralization" that can fulfill this desire, and David's rise to power through a careful building of alliances shows that he functioned as a chieftain. For the period of David's rise, "the archaeological and literary models suggest simultaneous processes of devolution and evolution similar to the symbioses among sedentary, semi-nomadic, and nomadic peoples documented in comparative sociology." The model of David "that is idealized—certainly not the only one remembered—portrays a pastoral nomad who rises to leadership among the Philistines, but successfully adapts to Benjaminite, Israelite, Judahite, Transjordanian, ruling class and peasant expectations and needs as well. Ideologically, however, his ideal role is that of a Yahwist pastoral nomadic chieftain and a former 'apiru who adapts to the needs and aspirations of all segments within the system" (288, 291).[18]

Finally, Flanagan uses Roy A. Rappaport's "systemic ecological model of religion" to illuminate features of Yahwism's role in David's rise to power. He suggests, for example, that religion performed an integrative function, legitimating a "dual . . . paramountcy for a single leader [and] enabl[ing] distinctive economic and social systems to remain intact while integrating Israel, Judah, and others politically" (311). But religion can also obstruct "the adjustments needed to accommodate the sociopolitical aspirations to the new ecological realities." The David stories provide evidence for this in the prohibition against temple-building, which "accurately reflects the socioeconomic setting of the period as well as segmented groups' predisposition against centralization." In Nathan's oracle to David (2 Samuel 7) we have "a sacred message prohibiting [a] temple and establishing [a] non-monarchic Davidic dynasty [which] is linked to an ultimate sacred egalitarian proposition" (309, 314–15).

We turn now to Frick's monograph on the origins of the Israelite state, which focuses largely on archaeological evidence and "proceeds under the assumption that data and theories from the social sciences, especially anthropology, can and do provide the biblical scholar suggestive and illuminating controlled comparisons between many of the sociopolitical processes which were at work in early Israel and similar processes which were operative elsewhere" (1985, 9). His argument proceeds through four stages.

Since the problem is to understand the nature of the social change that occurred in the transition to monarchy in Israel, the first step is to review theories of cultural evolution.[19] Frick favors an approach to "sociocultural evolution [that] takes as its starting point the idea of

ecological succession, where succession is 'a descriptive term referring to the classification of ecological systems in terms of increasing
complexity over time'" (20). R. N. Adams postulates "a fundamental
growth sequence that repeats itself through the course of human
social evolution . . . [and] consists of three phases: identity, coordina-
tion, and centralization." This "model of evolution" is "compatible
with the concept of ecological succession" (21–22). Frick also reviews
several types of theories about state formation and makes an important distinction between "pristine" and "secondary" states (one of "the
significant variables" in the formation of the latter "is the cultural contact of a non-state entity with a state entity"; 32). The Israelite monarchy developed as a "secondary state."

The processes that set pristine and secondary states in motion may
differ, and Frick describes several "systemic explanatory models of secondary state formation" (32). In general, these focus on social and ecological variables, such as the institutions "responsible for the capture or
harnessing, storage, distribution and flow of energy within and
between populations" (B. Price), and "variations in agricultural risk,
diversity, and productivity, as well as . . . the size and character of the
environment" (W. T. Sanders and D. Webster). Of particular importance is "catastrophe theory" (R. Thom, C. Renfrew), according to
which "sudden changes or discontinuities in a sociocultural system are
produced by and can be understood in terms of altogether gradual and
continuous changes in the control variables within that system." System
collapse results in "the emergence of segmentary societies, followed by
the subsequent regeneration of a chiefdom and/or secondary state society" (43, 49). The trajectory Frick suggests "for ancient Israel is one
that runs from state to segmentary society (with the collapse of the
Canaanite city-state system), from segmentary society to chiefdom (at
least by the time of Saul), and from chiefdom to state (David in
Jerusalem)" (50).

Employing comparative material from the ethnography of African
societies, the second stage in the argument is to show that early Israel
can be understood as a segmentary society.[20] Such societies are
"'acephalous . . ., i.e. not politically organized by a central court.'"
Rather, their "'political organization is established by multi-graded
groups which are politically of equal rank and similarly classified'" (52;
quoting C. Sigrist). Such societies are characterized by a "balance of
power between segments" (55) and are susceptible to fissioning and
the realignment of segments. B. Lindars' analysis of Judges reveals "the
kind of fluidity that is typical of a segmentary society" (62).

Eventually, "agricultural intensification in the Palestinian environment" led to "the transformation of a segmentary lineage system into a chiefdom" (66). One problem with segmentary societies is that they lack mechanisms (such as citizenship) to incorporate large numbers of outsiders. "Chiefdom [is] a socio-cultural adaptive device in early Israel which enabled the incorporation process" (69).

In the third stage in his argument, which makes little explicit reference to Israel, Frick examines the characteristics of chiefdoms. Anthropological studies indicate that two organizational principles are basic to chiefdoms: "(1) ranking of individual statuses within the local community; and (2) the regionally centralized organization of local communities." While chiefdoms do not abolish previously existing segments, they keep their "built-in tendencies to fission" in check (1985, 76). Comparative materials also identify important dimensions that define and legitimate the chief's leadership. Prominent among the latter is the chief's function as a redistributor of wealth, through which individuals become dependent on him and the power of lineage heads is undermined. Religion helps establish "a sense of common identity and unified political action among a collection of autonomous groups" (82). Warfare is significant "in its ability to negate evolutionary constraints, like population growth and resource limitation, and it enhances the chief's role as redistributor. Clientship is important, since the total group of clients is a chief's power base (78–86).

In this context Frick discusses proposals by anthropological archaeologists working in several parts of the globe that certain archaeological features can be taken as diagnostic of chiefdoms. Among these are evidence that the society was ranked, demographic data (evidence of site hierarchies and central places), and evidence for cooperative production and strategies for dealing with the environment (for example, relating to agricultural practices; 86–97).

In the final stage of his argument, Frick presents a lengthy discussion of agriculture and social organization in which he attempts "to delineate for ancient Israel what was involved in the process of translating ecological potential into sociopolitical change" (100). He describes the agricultural environment of the Palestinian hill country and discusses the development of technologies—like terracing, cisterns, and the use of iron tools—the primary significance of which was that they "enabled the intensification of settlement in an area in which the obstacles to productive agriculture were many" (130). For example, terraces, which were attached to villages and existed prior to the formation of an Israelite state, not only reduced runoff, but also buffered a segmentary society's tendency to fission by encouraging cooperative labor at planting and harvest and also "fixed socioeconomic relations within and between villages" (137). He describes archaeological evidence for chiefdom at Tel Masos southeast of Beersheba, including evidence that society was ranked and that the village was itself "a central site in the area" (161) and he suggests a role for religion in maintaining "social solidarity and law and order on the village and inter-village level and [making] possible multicommunity groupings in pre-state Israel" (165–66).

What Frick does is "look at early Israel in a holistic way as an information system or an adaptive system that enabled the survival of the new cultural entity Israel in Iron I Palestine and through 'adaptive modification' led to the political entity of the state, the Davidic monarchy" (193). In this developmental process, "when labor needs required a level of efficiency beyond that which could be supplied by productive specialization in the local household or residential group, an organizing principle based on the hierarchical partitioning of society emerged and the chiefdom appeared" (199). Paramount chiefs like Saul and David were "a most effective way in which to monitor matter and energy exchanges and the deviation of relevant variables over a large area" (203).

The narratives in the books of Samuel relate in a series of anecdotes how David rose to power and in the process united various Palestinian factions. The studies of Frick and Flanagan move the account of this development out of the realm of history-as-biography and focus our attention on the social and political dynamics of this period of transition.

CONCLUSION

In a companion volume in this series written more than a decade ago, Robert Wilson noted that "the use of social-scientific data in biblical studies is now in its infancy" (1984, 81). The number and variety of articles and books that have appeared in the intervening years suggest that this approach is on its way to becoming a standard tool in the repertoire of biblical scholars.

Modern biblical scholarship has been resolutely pluralistic. Methodologies are continually developed and refined—one has only to scan the titles in this series to be reminded of the scope of these efforts— but seldom used in isolation. So it is with anthropological approaches to the Hebrew Bible, which as we have seen in the examples discussed in this book, can be used in conjunction with other approaches to arrive at a more nuanced interpretation of certain texts. For the biblical scholar anthropology is a useful partner, not a panacea.

The main impetus for forming such a partnership is that we encounter things in the Hebrew Bible—among them resuscitation, divination, and other matters discussed in this book—that we fail to

97

grasp because of the paucity of information about them in the texts or because they are foreign to our own experience and way of looking at the world. That one's world view predisposes one to a particular under-standing and hides, so to speak, others is graphically illustrated by the problem posed in the essay by Ernst Wendland to which I referred at the end of chapter 2: How can one translate the Elijah and Elisha nar-ratives so as to protect against the natural inclination of Tonga readers to see these two figures as witch doctors and to foster a reading more in harmony with the Western Christian interpretation?

A value judgment underlying the use of anthropological theories and materials in biblical studies is that we need to avoid ethnocentrism as much as possible, recognizing that world views different from our own have a logic of their own. We cannot simply categorize such societies as "prescientific" or the like and seek to explain away their characteristic features in terms more at home in modern Western thought. Here anthropology offers the reader of the Hebrew Bible hope and help by providing analogies that will suggest a richer understanding of the bib-lical text. Since ethnographies in particular are often quite interesting, this book may perhaps be considered an invitation to biblical scholars to read anthropology for fun and profit.

NOTES

1. Two other quintessentially Deuteronomistic texts, commenting on the reasons for the fall of northern Israel and the sins of the Judean king Manasseh, list multiple types of divination, connect it with child sacrifice, and see both as among those foreign practices that have been adopted in infringement of Yah-weh's law (2 Kgs. 17:17, 21:6).

2. Cf. 1 Sam. 6:2, Jer. 27:9; Babylonian divination is mentioned in Ezek. 21:18–23 (MT 23–28).

3. Cryer argues that some forms of Israelite divination, such as dream inter-pretation (263–72) and the so–called "priestly oracle" (286–95), display Mesopotamian features, and he shows "that the late first-millennium Assyro-Babylonian 'queries/reports' tradition provided the formal background for the descriptions in Judges and Samuel of the various ominous consultations which there take place" (295–305; the quotation is from 304). Horowitz and Hurowitz (1992) suggest on the basis of an Akkadian text a Mesopotamian origin for the Urim and Thummim. The Deuteronomists' rejection of divination as a practice of Israel's Canaanite neighbors may be ideological, but the Israelites' recourse to divination was clearly in harmony with their larger Near Eastern environment.

4. So Horowitz and Hurowitz 1992. For a discussion of lot-casting, cf. Lind-blom 1962, and for other views on the Urim and Thummim, Robertson 1964 and Cryer 1994, 293–96.

5. The criterion of fulfillment, whether of divination or of prophecy, is noto-

riously difficult to employ. What exactly constitutes fulfillment in a given case? How long should one wait before passing judgment? Note, for example, the series of "inquiries" recounted in Judges 20:18–28. On the basis of the response to their divination, the Israelites could reasonably have expected success in their first battle, or the second. The original response proved inaccurate twice before being "fulfilled" on the third occasion. In addition, rationalizations are always available. For example, if one asks a diviner, "Shall I go up to such and such a place?," receives an affirmative answer, and then encounters misfortune during the journey, one could be consoled by the conviction that things would have been worse if one had not gone. Cryer goes so far as to argue that acts of divination "are not logically related to one another in any sort of system," and "have nothing to do with 'predicting the future' in our sense'" (1994, 117–23). Bascom (1941) provides a particularly good discussion of reasons why people might continue to have confidence in diviners despite mistaken predictions.

6. For a more detailed discussion of the points made in this and the following two paragraphs, see Overholt 1989, 137–40, and the references cited there.

7. The interchange between diviner and client may be highly formalized and proceed quite rapidly. Meyer (1991, 98) reports Lobi consultations "may average a total of eight hundred to a thousand questions" and be completed in "about forty-five minutes."

8. Peek (1991b) argues that "divination systems temporarily shift decision making into a liminal realm by emphatically participating in opposing cognitive modes" in order to effect "a dynamic reassessment of customs and values in the face of an ever-changing world" (193, 195). It is in the dialogue between diviner and client "that the unique synthesis of cognitive modes occurs" (203). Participants are shaken out of their current inadequate "understanding of the situation" and moved toward the formulation of a plan of action. "All types of divination aid decision making by literally re-viewing the problem in light of different knowledge (whatever its source), and then the process integrates this perspective with contemporary reality by means of discussion between diviner and client" (206).

9. See also Rigby 1975, 134–35 (Kiganda, Uganda) and Hammond-Tooke 1955 (Baca, South Africa).

10. For example, the Bunyoro of Uganda (Beattie 1964) and traditional Japan (Blacker 1981).

11. See the references in Overholt 1989, 139–40. Lester Grabbe argues that one of the important things the anthropological study of "religious specialists" teaches us is that "in most societies there is a certain amount of overlap and blurring of [their] roles" (1993, 45), and he cites evidence that this was also true in ancient Israel.

12. To illustrate this with an example from the philosophical discussion of performatives, the words "I pronounce you man and wife" actually perform an action, but only if uttered in the appropriate social context.

13. Here Meyers draws on the theoretical discussions of M. Z. Rosaldo and S. C. Rogers. Based on her observations of life in a peasant village in southern France, Rogers develops the notion of the "myth of male dominance." The

"characteristics of a system in which [this myth] is operative . . . can be identified in a wide variety of peasant and even nonpeasant societies" (42–44).

14. "[T]he centrality of the household in prestate Israel emerges as a critical factor in determining gender relations. When the household occupies the preeminent place in a society, women have a strong role in decision making and consequently exercise considerable power in the household" (174).

15. Cf. also Carol Meyers, "The Drum-Dance-Song Ensemble: Women's Performance in Biblical Israel" (pp. 49–67 in Kimberly Marshall, ed., *Rediscovering the Muses: Women's Musical Traditions*, Boston: Northeastern University Press, 1993). Meyers again uses a multidisciplinary approach, combining data from the biblical text, archaeology, and anthropology (in particular from folklore and ethnomusicology) to identify "a distinct tradition of women's performance" and to draw inferences from this tradition about the status of women in ancient Israelite society.

16. Flanagan (1988) and Frick (1985). See also Flanagan (1981).

17. "Comparative sociology" includes both anthropology and sociology, though in his study Flanagan draws mostly on the first of these disciplines (cf. 1988, 22). To a much greater extent than the following brief summary can indicate, he discusses and makes use of the work of E. Leach, M. Harris, R. Rappaport, L. Holy and M. Stuchlik, and V. Turner in developing his own models for interpreting the data.

18. Flanagan cites the rise to power of King Ibn Saud of modern Arabia as a diachronic analogue to the process of centralization in the Davidic Iron Age. Among other things, the two shared strategies in warfare, using marriage to form alliances, and the redistribution of wealth. Both shunned the title "king" and faced "pressures toward centralization . . . [that were] balanced by those against" (for example, Yahwist and Wahhabi iconoclasm; 1988, 306–07). Comparing episodes in the stories of Ibn Saud and David, however, "proves neither the latter's historicity nor the motives of the storytellers. Even an overall pattern of similarity does not confirm Davidic history. It is the relationships and tensions in Ibn Saud's and David's stories, and how the former illumines the coherence and interference in ancient sources, that is important" (1988, 337).

19. For another discussion of "evolutionary paradigms and state formation studies," see Frick 1986, 17–26.

20. For a discussion of sources for and the use of African ethnographic materials, see Frick 1986, 26–32.

Bibliography

Andrzejewski, B. W.
   1974 "The Veneration of Sufi Saints and Its Impact on the Oral Literature of the Somali People and on Their Literature in Arabic." *African Language Studies* 15:15–53.
Anisimov, A. F.
   1963 "The Shaman's Tent of the Evenks and the Origin of the Shamanistic Rite." In *Studies in Siberian Shamanism*, edited by H. N. Michael, 84–123. Toronto: Arctic Institute of North America.
Atkinson, Jane Monnig
   1987 "The Effectiveness of Shamans in an Indonesian Ritual." *American Anthropologist* 89:342–55.
Bailey, L. R.
   1985 "Death." In *Harper's Bible Dictionary*, edited by Paul J. Achtemeier, 213–14. San Francisco: Harper and Row.
Barrett, Stanley R.
   1984 *The Rebirth of Anthropological Theory*. Toronto: University of Toronto Press.
Barton, John
   1986 *Oracles of God: Perceptions of Ancient Prophecy in Israel After the Exile*. London: Darton, Longman and Todd.
Bascom, William R.
   1941 "The Sanctions of Ifa Divination." *Journal of the Royal Anthropological Institute* 71:43–54.
   1967 "Two Forms of Afro-Cuban Divination." In *Acculturation in the Americas*, edited by Sol Tax, 169–79. New York: Cooper Square.
   1969 *Ifa Divination: Communication Between Gods and Men in West Africa*. Bloomington: Indiana University Press.
Beattie, John
   1964 "Divination in Bunyoro, Uganda." *Sociologus* n.s. 14:44–62.
Belsey, Catherine
   1980 *Critical Practice*. London: Routledge.
Benedict, Ruth
   1935 *Zuni Mythology*, vols. 1 and 2. New York: Columbia University Press.
Bergen, Wesley
   1992a "The Prophetic Alternative: Elisha and the Israelite Monarchy." In *Elijah and Elisha in Socioliterary Perspective*, edited by Robert B. Coote, 127–37. Atlanta: Scholars Press.

1992b "2 Kings 4:8–37 and the Discourse of the Dominant." Paper presented at the annual meeting of the Society of Biblical Literature, San Francisco, November 1992.

Blacker, Carmen
1981 "Japan." In *Oracles and Divination,* edited by Michael Loewe and Carmen Blacker, 63–86. Boulder: Shambhala.

Bledstein, Adrien Janis
1992 "Was *Habbirya* a Healing Ritual Performed by a Woman in King David's House?" *Biblical Research* 37:15–31.

Blier, Rudolph
1991 "Diviners as Alienists and Annunciators among the Batammaliba of Togo." In *African Divination Systems,* edited by Philip M. Peek, 73–90. Bloomington: Indiana University Press.

Bloch-Smith, Elizabeth M.
1992 "The Cult of the Dead in Judah: Interpreting the Material Remains." *Journal of Biblical Literature* 111:213–24.

Bronner, Leah
1968 *The Stories of Elijah and Elisha as Polemics Against Baal Worship.* Leiden: E. J. Brill.

Brotzman, Ellis R.
1988 "Man and the Meaning of *nepes.*" *Bibliotheca Sacra* 145:400–09.

Callaway, Henry
1991 "The Initiation of a Zulu Diviner." In *African Divination Systems,* edited by Philip M. Peek, 27–35. Bloomington: Indiana University Press.

Carroll, Robert P.
1986 *Jeremiah: A Commentary.* Philadelphia: Westminster Press.
1989 "Prophecy and Society." In *The World of Ancient Israel,* edited by R. E. Clements, 203–25. Cambridge, England: Cambridge University Press.
1991 "Textual Strategies and Ideology in the Second Temple Period." In *Second Temple Studies: 1. Persian Period,* edited by Philip R. Davies, 108–24. Sheffield, England: JSOT Press.

Colby, Benjamin N., and Lore M. Colby
1981 *The Daykeeper: The Life and Discourse of an Ixil Diviner.* Cambridge, Mass.: Harvard University Press.

Coote, Robert B.
1992 *Elijah and Elisha in Socioliterary Perspective.* Atlanta: Scholars Press.

Coote, Robert B. and Keith W. Whitelam
1987 *The Emergence of Early Israel in Historical Perspective.* Sheffield, England: Almond.

Cryer, Frederick H.
1994 *Divination in Ancient Israel and Its Near Eastern Environment: A Socio-Historical Investigation.* Sheffield, England: JSOT Press.

Culley, Robert
1980 "Punishment Stories in the Legends of the Prophets." In *Orientation by Disorientation,* edited by R. A. Spencer, 167–81. Pittsburgh: Pickwick.

Devisch, Rene
   1991 "Mediumistic Divination among the Northern Yaka of Zaire: Etiology and Ways of Knowing." In *African Divination Systems*, edited by Philip M. Peek, 112-32. Bloomington: Indiana University Press.
Dornan, S. S.
   1923 "Divination and Divining Bones." *South African Journal of Science* 20:504–11.
Elwin, Verrier
   1955 *The Religion of an Indian Tribe*. Oxford: Oxford University Press.
Feeley-Harnik, Gillian
   1982 "Is Historical Anthropology Possible? The Case of the Runaway Slave." In *Humanizing America's Iconic Book*, edited by Gene M. Tucker and Douglas A. Knight, 95–126. Chico, Calif.: Scholars Press.
Fiensy, D.
   1987 "Using the Nuer Culture of Africa in Understanding the Old Testament: An Evaluation." *Journal for the Study of the Old Testament* 38:73–83.
Firth, Raymond
   1969 "Foreword." In *Spirit Mediumship and Society in Africa*, edited by John Beattie and John Middleton, ix–xiv. London: Routledge and Kegan Paul.
Flanagan, James W.
   1981 "Chiefs in Israel." *Journal for the Study of the Old Testament* 20:47–73.
   1988 *David's Social Drama: A Hologram of Israel's Early Iron Age*. Sheffield, England: Almond.
Fohrer, Georg
   1957 *Elia*. Zurich: Zwingli-Verlag.
Frick, Frank S.
   1985 *The Formation of the State in Ancient Israel*. Sheffield, England: Almond.
   1986 "Social Science Methods and Theories of Significance for the Study of the Israelite Monarchy: A Critical Review Essay." *Semeia* 37:9–52.
Garbett, G. Kingsley
   1966 "Religious Aspects of Political Succession among the Valley Korekore." In *The Zambesian Past*, edited by Eric Stokes and Richard Brown, 137–70. Manchester: Manchester University Press.
   1969 "Spirit Mediums as Mediators in Valley Korekore Society." In *Spirit Mediumship and Society in Africa*, edited by John Beattie and John Middleton, 104–27. London: Routledge and Kegan Paul.
Geertz, Clifford
   1973 *Thick Description: Toward an Interpretive Theory of Culture*. New York: Basic Books.
   1983 *Local Knowledge: Further Essays in Interpretive Anthropology*. New York: Basic Books.

CULTURAL ANTHROPOLOGY AND THE OLD TESTAMENT

Giddens, Anthony
    1987 *Social Theory and Modern Sociology*. Stanford, Calif.: Stanford University Press.
Gifford, E. W.
    1934 "The Cocopa." *University of California Publications in American Archaeology and Ethnology* 31:257–334.
Goldammer, K.
    1972 "Elemente des Schamanismus im alten Testament." *Ex Orbe Religionum: Studies in the History of Religions* (Supplements to *Numen* 21–22), 266–85.
Gottwald, Norman, edited by
    1986 *Social Scientific Criticism of the Hebrew Bible and Its Social World: The Israelite Monarchy*. Semeia 37.
Grabbe, Lester L.
    1993 "Prophets, Priests, Diviners and Sages in Ancient Israel." In *Of Prophets' Visions and the Wisdom of Sages*, edited by Heather A. McKay and David J. A. Clines, 43–62. Sheffield, England: JSOT Press.
Haeberlin, Herman K.
    1918 "Sbetetda'q, a Shamanistic Performance of the Coast Salish." *American Anthropologist* 20:249–57.
Hajdú, P.
    1968 "The Classification of Samoyed Shamans." In *Popular Beliefs and Folklore Tradition in Siberia*, edited by V. Dioszegi, 147–73. Bloomington: Indiana University Press, Uralic and Altaic Series, vol. 57.
Halifax, Joan
    1979 *Shamanic Voices: A Survey of Visionary Narratives*. New York: E. P. Dutton.
Hallowell, A. I.
    1942 *The Role of Conjuring in Saulteaux Society*. Philadelphia: University of Pennsylvania Press.
    1967 *Culture and Experience*. New York: Schocken.
Hammond-Tooke, William D.
    1955 "The Initiation of a Bhaca Isangoma Diviner." *African Studies* 14:16–22.
Haur, Chris, Jr.
    1987 "Anthropology in Historiography." *Journal for the Study of the Old Testament* 39:15–21.
Hentschel, Georg
    1977 *Die Elijaerzälungen*. Leipzig: St. Benno-Verlag.
Hill, Scott D.
    1992 "The Local Hero in Palestine in Comparative Perspective." In *Elijah and Elisha in Socioliterary Perspective*, edited by Robert B. Coote, 37–73. Atlanta: Scholars Press.
Horowitz, Wayne, and Victor (Avigdor) Hurowitz
    1992 "Urim and Thummim in Light of Psephomancy Ritual from Assur

104

(*LKA* 137)." *Journal of the Ancient Near Eastern Society* 21:95–115.

Hultkrantz, Åke

1957 *The North American Indian Orpheus Tradition: A Contribution to Comparative Religion*. Stockholm: Ethnographical Museum of Sweden.

1978 "Ecological and Phenomenological Aspects of Shamanism." In *Shamanism in Siberia*, edited by V. Dioszegi and M. Hoppal, 27–58. Budapest: Akademiai Kiado.

1992 *Shamanic Healing and Ritual Drama: Health and Medicine in Native North American Religious Traditions*. New York: Crossroad.

Irvin, Dorothy

1978 *Mytharion: The Comparison of Tales from the Old Testament and the Ancient Near East*. Neukirchen-Vluyn: Neukirchener Verlag.

Jenness, Diamond

1935 *The Ojibwa Indians of Parry Island, Their Social and Religious Life*. Ottawa: Canada Department of Mines, Bulletin 78, National Museum of Canada Anthropological Series No. 17.

Jobling, David

1991 "Text and the World—An Unbridgeable Gap? A Response to Carroll, Hoglund and Smith." In *Second Temple Studies: 1. Persian Period*, edited by Philip R. Davies, 175–82. Sheffield, England: JSOT Press.

Johnson, Aubrey R.

1964 *The Vitality of the Individual in the Thought of Ancient Israel*. 2d ed.; Cardiff: University of Wales Press.

Jones, William

1919 *Ojibwa Texts*. Part 2. Leyden and New York: American Ethnological Society.

Kapelrud, Arvid S.

1967 "Shamanistic Features in the Old Testament." In *Studies in Shamanism*, edited by Carl-Martin Edsman, 90–96. Stockholm: Almqvist and Wiksell.

Kilian, Rudolf

1966 "Die Totenerweckungen Elias und Elisas—eine Motivwanderung?" *Biblische Zeitschrift* 10:44–56.

Kirkpatrick, Patricia G.

1988 *The Old Testament and Folklore Study*. Sheffield, England: JSOT Press.

Knibb, Michael A.

1989 "Life and Death in the Old Testament." In *The World of Ancient Israel*, edited by R. E. Clements, 395–415. Cambridge, England: Cambridge University Press.

Kracke, Waud H.

1992 "He Who Dreams: The Nocturnal Source of Transforming Power in Kagwahiv Shamanism." In *Portals of Power: Shamanism in South America*, edited by E. Jean Matteson Langdon and Gerhard Baer, 127–48. Albuquerque: University of New Mexico Press.

LaFargue, Michael
    1988 "Are Texts Determinate? Derrida, Barth, and the Role of the Biblical
        Scholar." *Harvard Theological Review* 81: 341–57.
Lame Deer, John (Fire), and Richard Erdoes
    1972 *Lame Deer Seeker of Visions: The Life of a Sioux Medicine Man*. New
        York: Simon and Schuster.
Langdon, E. Jean Matteson
    1992a "Introduction: Shamanism and Anthropology." In *Portals of Power:
        Shamanism in South America*, edited by E. Jean Matteson Langdon
        and Gerhard Baer, 1–21. Albuquerque: University of New Mexico
        Press.
    1992b "Dau: Shamanic Power in Siona Religion and Medicine." In *Portals
        of Power: Shamanism in South America*, edited by E. Jean Matteson
        Langdon and Gerhard Baer, 41–61. Albuquerque: University of New
        Mexico Press.
Langdon, E. Jean Matteson, and Gerhard Baer
    1992 *Portals of Power: Shamanism in South America*. Albuquerque: Uni-
        versity of New Mexico Press.
Leenhardt, Jacques
    1980 "Toward a Sociology of Reading." In *The Reader in the Text*, edited by
        Susan R. Suleiman and Inge Crosman, 205–24. Princeton: Princeton
        University Press.
Lessa, William A., and Evon Z. Vogt
    1965 *Reader in Comparative Religion: An Anthropological Approach*. 2nd
        ed. New York: Harper and Row.
Lewis, I. M.
    1986 *Religion in Context: Cults and Charisma*. Cambridge, England: Cam-
        bridge University Press.
Lewis, Theodore J.
    1989 *Cults of the Dead in Ancient Israel and Ugarit*. Atlanta: Scholars Press.
Lindblom, J.
    1962 *Prophecy in Ancient Israel*. Oxford: Basil Blackwell.
Logan, Brad
    1980 "The Ghost Dance among the Paiute: An Ethnohistorical View of the
        Documentary Evidence 1889–1893." *Ethnohistory* 27:267–88.
Long, Burke O.
    1975 "The Social Setting for Prophetic Miracle Stories." *Semeia* 3:46–63.
    1984 *1 Kings, With an Introduction to Historical Literature*. Grand Rapids:
        Eerdmans.
    1991 *2 Kings*. Grand Rapids: Eerdmans.
Lopatin, Ivan A.
    1946–49 "A Shamanistic Performance for a Sick Boy." *Anthropos* 4:153–74.
Lowie, R. H.
    1924 "Notes on Shoshonean Ethnography." *Anthropological Papers of the
        American Museum of Natural History* 20 (3) 183–314.

McClelland, E. M.
    1982 *The Cult of Ifa Among the Yoruba.* Vol. 1, *Folk Practice and the Art.*
        London: Ethnographica.
McNutt, Paula M.
    1990 *The Forging of Israel: Iron Technology, Symbolism, and Tradition in
        Ancient Society.* Sheffield, England: Almond.
Merkur, Daniel
    1985 *Becoming Half Hidden: Shamanism and Initiation Among the Inuit.*
        Stockholm: Almqvist & Wiksell International.
Meyer, Piet
    1991 "Divination among the Lobi of Burkina Faso." In *African Divination
        Systems,* edited by Philip M. Peek, 91–99. Bloomington: Indiana
        University Press.
Meyers, Carol
    1988 *Discovering Eve: Ancient Israelite Women in Context.* New York:
        Oxford University Press.
Mikhailovskii, V. M.
    1895 "Shamanism in Siberia and European Russia." *Journal of the Royal
        Anthropological Institute of Great Britain and Ireland* 24: 62–100,
        126–58.
Murphy, Jane M.
    1964 "Psychotherapeutic Aspects of Shamanism on St. Lawrence Island,
        Alaska." In *Magic, Faith, and Healing: Studies in Primitive Psychia-
        try Today,* edited by Ari Kiev, 53–83. Glencoe, Ill.: Free Press.
Nadel, S.F.
    1946 "A Study of Shamanism in the Nuba Mountains." *Journal of the Royal
        Anthropological Institute* 76:25–37.
Niditch, Susan
    1987 *Underdogs and Tricksters: A Prelude to Biblical Folklore.* San Fran-
        cisco: Harper and Row.
Oppenheim, A. Leo
    1964 *Ancient Mesopotamia.* Chicago: University of Chicago Press.
Ortner, Sherry
    1984 "Theory in Anthropology Since the Sixties." *Comparative Studies in
        Society and History* 26:126–66.
Overholt, Thomas W.
    1986 *Prophecy in Cross-Cultural Perspective.* Atlanta: Scholars Press.
    1989 *Channels of Prophecy: The Social Dynamics of Prophetic Activity.*
        Minneapolis: Fortress Press.
Overholt, Thomas W., and J. Baird Callicott
    1982 *Clothed-in-Fur and Other Tales: An Introduction to an Ojibwa World
        View.* Washington, D.C.: University Press of America.
Park, Willard Z.
    1938 *Shamanism in Western North America: A Study in Cultural Relation-
        ships.* Evanston, Ill.: Northwestern University Press.

Parker, Simon B.
1978 "Possession Trance and Prophecy in Pre-Exilic Israel." *Vetus Testamentum* 28:271–85.

Pecirkova, Jana
1985 "Divination and Politics in the Late Assyrian Empire." *Archiv Orientalni* 53:155–68.

Peek, Philip M.
1991a "Introduction: The Study of Divination, Present and Past." In *African Divination Systems*, edited by Philip M. Peek, 1–22. Bloomington: Indiana University Press.
1991b "African Divination Systems: Non-Normal Modes of Cognition." In *African Divination Systems*, 193–212.

Petersen, David L.
1981 *The Roles of Israel's Prophets*. Sheffield, England: JSOT Press.

Phillips, Gary A.
1990 "Exegesis as Critical Praxis: Reclaiming History and Text From a Postmodern Perspective." *Semeia* 51:7–49.

Pollock, Donald
1992 "Culina Shamanism: Gender, Power, and Knowledge." In *Portals of Power: Shamanism in South America*, edited by E. Jean Matteson Langdon and Gerhard Baer, 25–40. Albuquerque: University of New Mexico Press.

Porteous, N. W.
1962 "The Prophets and the Problem of Continuity." In *Israel's Prophetic Heritage*, edited by B. W. Anderson and W. Harrelson, 11–25. New York: Harper.

Powers, William K.
1977 *Oglala Religion*. Lincoln: University of Nebraska Press.

Rentería, Tamis Hoover
1992 "The Elijah/Elisha Stories: A Socio-cultural Analysis of Prophets and the People in Ninth-Century B.C.E. Israel." In *Elijah and Elisha in Socioliterary Perspective*, edited by Robert B. Coote, 75–126. Atlanta: Scholars Press.

Rigby, Peter
1975 "Prophets, Diviners, and Prophetism: The Recent History of Kiganda Religion." *Journal of Anthropological Research* 31:116–48.

Rigby, Peter and F. Lule
1971 *Divination and Healing in Peri-Urban Kampala, Uganda*. Kampala, Uganda: Makerere Institute of Social Research.

Robertson, E.
1964 "The Urim and Thummim; What Were They?" *Vetus Testamentum* 14:67–74.

Rofé, Alexander
1988 *The Prophetical Stories: The Narratives about the Prophets in the Hebrew Bible, Their Literary Types and History*. Jerusalem: Magnes Press.

Rogerson, John W.

1978 *Anthropology and the Old Testament*. Atlanta: John Knox Press.

1989 "Anthropology and the Old Testament." In *The World of Ancient Israel*, edited by R.E. Clements, 17–37. Cambridge, England: Cambridge University Press.

Samuel, Geoffrey

1990 *Mind, Body and Culture: Anthropology and the Biological Interface*. Cambridge, England: Cambridge University Press.

Schaeffer, Claude E.

1969 *Blackfoot Shaking Tent*. Calgary, Alberta: Glenbow-Alberta Institute.

Schmitt, Armin

1975 "Die Totenerweckung in 2 Kon 4,8–37: Eine literaturwissenschaftliche Untersuchung." *Biblische Zeitschrift* 19:1–25.

1977 "Die Totenerweckung in 1 Kon. XVII 17–24: Eine form- und gattungskritische Untersuchung." *Vetus Testamentum* 27:454–74.

Shaw, Rosalind

1991 "Splitting Truths from Darkness: Epistemological Aspects of Temne Divination." In *African Divination Systems*, edited by Philip M. Peek, 137–52. Bloomington: Indiana University Press.

Shields, Mary E.

1993 "Subverting a Man of God, Elevating a Woman: Role and Power Reversals in 2 Kings 4." *Journal for the Study of the Old Testament* 58:59–69.

Shirokogoroff, S. M.

1935 *Psychomental Complex of the Tungus*. London: Kegan Paul, Trench, Trubner.

Siskin, Edgar E.

1983 *Washo Shamans and Peyotists: Religious Conflict in an American Indian Tribe*. Salt Lake City: University of Utah Press.

Smith, Harlan Ingersoll

1896 "Certain Shamanistic Ceremonies Among the Ojibwas." *American Antiquarian and Oriental Journal* 18:282–89.

Smith, Jonathan Z.

1978 *Map Is Not Territory: Studies in the History of Religions*. Leiden: Brill.

1982 *Imagining Religion: From Babylon to Jonestown*. Chicago: University of Chicago Press.

Smith, Mark S.

1990 *The Early History of God*. San Francisco: Harper and Row.

Speck, Frank G.

1977 *Naskapi: The Savage Hunters of the Labrador Peninsula*. Norman: University of Oklahoma Press.

Thompson, Stith

1955–58 *The Motif-Index of Folk-Literature*, 6 vols. Bloomington: Indiana University Press.

Todd, Judith A.
   1992 "The Pre-Deuteronomistic Elijah Cycle." In *Elijah and Elisha in Soci-oliterary Perspective*, edited by Robert B. Coote, 1–35. Atlanta: Scholars Press.
Turner, Victor
   1975 *Revelation and Divination in Ndembu Ritual*. Ithaca, N.Y.: Cornell University Press.
Vaux, Roland de
   1961 *Ancient Israel: Its Life and Institutions*. New York: McGraw-Hill.
Vollweiler, Lothar G., and Alison B. Sanchez
   1983 "Divination—'Adaptive' from Whose Perspective?" *Ethnology* 22:193–210.
Waghorne, Joanne Punzo
   1984 "From Geertz's Ethnography to an Ethnotheology?" In *Anthropology and the Study of Religion*, edited by Robert L. Moore and Frank E. Reynolds, 31–55. Chicago: Center for the Scientific Study of Religion.
Wendland, Ernst R.
   1992 "Elijah and Elisha: Sorcerers or Witch Doctors?" *Bible Translator* 43:213–23.
Whiting, Beatrice Blyth
   1950 *Paiute Sorcery*. New York: Viking Fund.
Whybray, R. N.
   1987 *The Making of the Pentateuch: A Methodological Study*. Sheffield, England: JSOT Press.
Wilson, Robert R.
   1979 "Prophecy and Ecstasy: A Reexamination." *Journal of Biblical Literature* 98: 321–37.
   1980 *Prophecy and Society in Ancient Israel*. Philadelphia: Fortress Press.
   1984 *Sociological Approaches to the Old Testament*. Philadelphia: Fortress Press.
Wright, Pablo
   1992 "Dream, Shamanism, and Power among the Toba of Formosa Province." In *Portals of Power: Shamanism in South America*, edited by E. Jean Matteson Langdon and Gerhard Baer, 149–72. Albuquerque: University of New Mexico Press.
Würthwein, Ernst
   1989 "Zur Opferprobe Elias I Reg 18,21–39." In *Prophet und Prophetenbuch*, edited by Volkmar Fritz, K.-F. Pohlmann, und H.-C. Schmitt, 277–84. Berlin: De Gruyter.

Index of Biblical References

Index of Modern Authors